# Most Guys Are Losers
## (And How to Find a Winner)

## Dating Wit & Wisdom from Your Dad

# MARK BERZINS

## Illustrated by Marc Huebert

authorHOUSE®

AuthorHouse™
1663 Liberty Drive
Bloomington, IN 47403
www.authorhouse.com
Phone: 1 (800) 839-8640

Published by AuthorHouse 04/16/2015

ISBN: 978-1-5049-0540-4 (sc)
ISBN: 978-1-5049-0541-1 (e)

Print information available on the last page.

Any people depicted in stock imagery provided by Thinkstock are models, and such images are being used for illustrative purposes only. Certain stock imagery © Thinkstock.

This book is printed on acid-free paper.

Because of the dynamic nature of the Internet, any web addresses or links contained in this book may have changed since publication and may no longer be valid. The views expressed in this work are solely those of the author and do not necessarily reflect the views of the publisher, and the publisher hereby disclaims any responsibility for them.

### *Praise for*
### Most Guys Are Losers

"This is the one book every mom should slip into her daughter's duffle bag before she leaves for college. It's the wisdom no one teaches in the classroom, but should: how to make smart dating choices that will lead to happiness. This is 'The Talk' every girl needs to hear, but won't listen to if it comes from her own parent!"

~ Rachel Greenwald, *New York Times* bestselling author of *Have Him at Hello: Confessions from 1,000 Guys About What Makes Them Fall in Love... Or Never Call Back* (translated into 16 languages)


"Remember the name Mark Berzins—he is as eloquent, passionate, informative, empowering, self-aware, funny, entertaining, and insightful as they come. He understands what makes men tick, what women want, and what all of us really need on our journey to find love and happiness.

~ Brian Howie, Producer of "The Great Love Debate" and Author of *How to Find Love in 60 Seconds*


"Mark and I were roommates at Stanford, and even then, he struck me as one of the only guys who understood chivalry. Plus, he is a man with a conscience, so he's not afraid to dish about the worst (and best) characteristics of the male species. *Most Guys Are Losers* will be required reading before my daughter heads to college."

~ Rich Barton, Founder, Expedia and Zillow

## Dedication

For my girls.

There are many important things in here which I would find difficult to discuss with you face-to-face. This made it easier.

## Who Am I and Why Should You Listen to Me?

"Most guys are losers."

Really? Is this possible? What do I know, anyway—
and why should anyone listen to me? Well, it turns
out that, besides being a dad who's crazy about his
three daughters, I am also uniquely qualified when it
comes to this particular subject. In fact, I've become
a reluctant expert over the years because I've had a
front-row seat to hundreds of relationship train wrecks.

I am one of the largest independent bar operators in
the country. On a daily basis for over 20 years, I have
worked with singles on both sides of my bars. I have
counseled innumerable people through just about
every relationship moment, good and bad. So while I
am not a credentialed relationship professional, believe
me when I tell you... I have seen it *ALL*.

Naturally, I like to see things work out, but I am not afraid to advocate for throwing in the towel, either. I am exactly the type of no-bullshit guy you would expect to find working in an industry full of single people who are looking for the "right" person. Many, many times I have seen firsthand the hurt and wreckage caused by a man's lack of caring and respect.

Because of this, I am one of the few guys willing to shoot you straight about other men. None of us are prone to pointing out our own shortcomings, especially to women... but the time has come. So, this book is not only for my daughters as they head off to college and the real world beyond, but also for the many single women out there searching for Mr. Right. I know you. I care about you. And I want to make you more aware of the Losers of this world—the ones who will waste your precious time and energy and ultimately break your heart.

Certainly, not all guys are Losers (yes, with a capital "L"), but plenty of them ARE. You need to be able to identify them—and then run the other way. So, let's get to know them. They come in all sizes and flavors, but I've started with the worst ones first. The Good Guys, I've left for last (and I'll tell you how to find them and how to keep them happy). Think of it this way—you have to eat your broccoli before you can dig into the ice cream.

Here's how this handbook is organized: It's bottoms up. I begin with the run-for-the-hills types and eventually bring you around to the man of your dreams. Yeah, it may seem a bit discouraging to tackle the subject of guys this way, but hang in there with me because I want you to be fully armed and fully aware. I promise you, once we finish with the Losers, the landscape just gets better and better—because the Good Guys *are* out there.

**Dad's Top 5 Ground Rules**

### <u>Rule #1</u>
**You Mean the World to Me**

No matter what happens in your romantic life, there will always be one man in your life who will love you no matter what—your father. Always know I am here for you. Be safe.

### <u>Rule #2</u>
**Don't Give Your Heart Away Too Soon**

Men are heartbreakers. That's why I wrote this book. Odds are good you will get hurt more than a few times before you find your champion. Keep your heart guarded until you are sure it is in good hands.

### Rule #3
### Trust Your Gut... and Trust Your Friends' Guts

Your instincts and those of the people who know and love you are almost never wrong. Trust yourself and them.

### Rule #4
### Don't Drink Too Much Around
### Men You Don't Know

Men, especially when you're drinking, are dangerous. Do not allow yourself to become incapacitated. In fact, don't get anywhere close. Have a few drinks, have fun, but *NEVER* overdo it. I cannot emphasize this enough.

### Rule #5
### Be Decisive and Then Be Strong

When you know he's not the one, end it right away. It only gets harder if you put it off. And once it's done, stick to your guns. Cut him out completely if need be, but don't fall back under his spell.

You are only young once and the dating pool is only going to get shallower for you. Keep seeking a good man, the right man.

# Part I

# <u>LOSERS</u>

*"How do women still go out with guys
when you consider the fact that
there is no greater threat to women than men?
Globally and historically, we're the #1 cause
of injury and mayhem to women.
We're the worst thing that ever happens to them."
— Louis CK*

*If you want to know how most men view women,
watch Eddie Murphy's 1987 concert film "Raw."
The part on cheating men is great
insight into the Loser mind.
— Your Dad*

"You know a bunch of single men. You must know a good man for me?"

I can't tell you how many terrific women I know who just assume I must know a good, single guy for them. I always tell them that I do know some great men who are single, but none that I would recommend for them to date. Ask *ANY* good guy you know the same question. You will get the same answer. For us, guys we like and guys we would like you to *DATE* are not pools which have a lot of overlap.

You see, being a relationship Loser doesn't always make him a complete loser among his buddies. We men *KNOW* when the guy we like to hang out with will be a disaster for *YOU* to hang out with. Our silence in response to the "what's he like?" queries from you should speak volumes. Most of our single friends are single for a reason. They are Losers when it comes to being a Winner for women.

For the purposes of this book, "Loser" is defined to mean "not worth your time." Some of the men identified in this section are *complete* losers, both as men *AND* as human beings. I would hope you'd have the sense to stay away from them to begin with. But other personality types in here are just Losers for the purposes of a relationship. They could be great people. They might be handsome. They might be charming. They might be brilliant. They might be rich. *BUT*, if they have traits or habits which fall under Part 1 of this book, they are almost certainly a Loser for you. Be their friend—just don't be their girlfriend... or wife!

Some of you may be reading this and realize you are already hitched to a Loser. That is a tough deal. Do yourself a favor. If he can't get his act together, and most Losers can't, it's time to move on. It is unlikely to ever get any better, so be the better person and just get it over with. A loveless, loser relationship is unfair to both of you.

It's hard, but you can do it—take it on, be decisive. If he's not the guy, then move along. The window of opportunity for Good Men gets smaller and smaller as you age, so there is no time to waste in a dead-end relationship. It's not easy to be so hard-nosed about it, but it is important. By the time you get to your 30s, the balance of power shifts very much in favor of single men... and even more of them are Losers at this point.

Part of what you, and all women, battle is your eternal optimism when it comes to finding Mr. Right. Women are just so incredibly hopeful about every guy they meet. But I feel like everyone heading out on a first date needs to do a reality check. Odds are, the guy you are about to spend the evening with is *NOT* Mr. Right. In fact, odds are very good you're going out with a Loser.

Of course, there are no statistical certainties in any of this. Most of my observations are generalizations. But a good rule of thumb is to always begin by assuming he's *NOT* Mr. Right... and then make him *PROVE* you wrong.

As I will show you, starting with this assumption is perfectly sensible... until he proves to be the exception!

Remember I told you I'd pull no punches? Well, this next section of the book may be a bit depressing in some ways... but it's absolutely necessary. We have to get the bad news out into the open. In the coming chapters, I'm going to cover so many kinds of Losers, you may think it's time to give up hope. But my purpose is not to render you hopeless. It is to make you aware... because once you are, you will be able to make much smarter choices.

As you meet new men, you will notice them falling into certain categories. And that will keep you from wasting your time... and *THAT* should give you hope. So read this section and come out the other side with your eyes wide open and your heart a more little guarded.

I'll kick off this section with the most serious Losers and their traits, all of which are dealbreakers, and work my way through to some lesser characteristics of Loserdom. Get through this, and it all gets better!

# **DEALBREAKERS**

## *(The Loser Top 10)*

*Lots of things can be fixed. Things can be fixed. But many times relationships between people cannot be fixed because they should not be fixed."*
*– C. JoyBell C.*

# #1

# THE ABUSER

*"One of the obstacles to recognizing
chronic mistreatment in relationships
is that most abusive men simply
don't seem like abusers."*
*– Lundy Bancroft*

*"An average of 28 percent of high
school and college students
experience dating violence at some point."*
*– Barrie Levy, In Love and In Danger*

They had just kissed in the car before rolling through the front door. She was on Cloud Nine.

"I think he could be the one," she whispered as they worked their way past the rail.

Kim was one of my favorites... heck, one of everyone's favorites. She was an amazing, happy person with a thousand-watt smile. Just about every guy in the bar looked forward to running into her just to be favored with one of those smiles. This guy, an airline pilot, had captured her heart pretty quickly. Kicking off the night with that kiss had pretty much sealed the deal.

They joined their party at the big corner table and, after the second round, were obviously having a great time together. He appeared to be a decent, normal guy, and they continued to dote on each other throughout the evening. Those of us on the other side of the bar were hopeful he might be the one to take Kim off the market for good. Things looked promising, and she certainly seemed hopeful.

Two weeks later he beat the crap out of her.

I think all of us wonder how a woman ends up in an abusive relationship, and the answer is often just like this. These guys can be very normal. Charming. Handsome. Even sincerely loving. But there is something wrong in their wiring that causes them to switch from Dr. Jekyll to Mr. Hyde... sometimes in just a flash. How can you possibly know?

In the pilot's case, the answer lay online. He had a record, and it was there to be found using some simple online tools. Not surprisingly, Kim blamed herself.

I assumed that it should go without saying that the number one dealbreaker for any relationship would be abuse of any kind. Then I read that domestic violence is the leading cause of injury to women between the ages of 15 and 44 in our country (*"Violence Against Women, A Majority Staff Report," Committee on the Judiciary, U.S. Senate, 102nd Congress, October 1992, pg 3*). That's more women than are injured in car accidents! Kim's situation was not unique. Tragically, it was fairly common.

But how can you know beforehand? In Kim's case, she didn't even see it coming. That means you find out when it is too late. The best you can do then is get away immediately and report it to the police.

But other women I have known in this situation have reflected on their experience and seen subtle signs before the blowup—an aggressive grab, a raised hand withdrawn, a warning through clenched teeth. Needless to say, if your guy ever seems to be restraining himself from violence toward you, it is already past time to get out.

Additionally, the Family Violence Prevention Fund reports that "having a verbally abusive partner is the variable 'most likely' to predict that a woman would be victimized by an intimate partner." Threats of violence or aggressive talk should be warning signs to pull the ripcord.

## The Bottom Line

If he comes anywhere near hurting you, or even threatens to hurt you, get away immediately. No second chances. No apologies accepted. These situations require clean and complete breaks. Avoid any contact after it is over and be sure to stick with a Wingwoman* if there's an occasion when you might run into The Abuser. Let your friends know what's going on so they can keep an eye out. Do not be afraid to go to the police and/or file for a restraining order. Better safe than sorry.

* Wingwoman is a take-off on the Air Force's "wingman," meaning the person who watches you and always has your back.

---

Way too many guys are Losers.

They will hurt you if you let them. Don't let them!

---

## #2

## THE CHEATER

*"People are always fascinated by infidelity because, in the end – whether we've had direct experience or not – there's a part of you that knows there's absolutely no more piercing betrayal."*
*– Junot Diaz*

*Percentage of men who say they would have an affair if they knew they would never get caught: 74%*
*— Journal of Marital and Family Therapy*

My first five years in the bar business, I worked with a terrific woman named Riley. When we first met, she was a newlywed and happy as could be... until she figured out her handsome, attorney husband was sleeping around on her. She came to work in a fury. "How could that asshole be cheating on me?!" Good question. She was one of the best people on my crew—sweet, funny, smart... and very pretty. "What does he think I am, an idiot?" Yes. He figured she'd never find out... or he just didn't care. Riley had married The Cheater. Turns out, she should have seen it coming... he had messed around on her when they were dating. Some things never change.

The Cheater is a character type that shows up early and often in a relationship. Commitments like "exclusive" or "married" really don't change the equation. The Cheater can't keep himself from straying, so understand that his pledge to you is not going to make any difference.

Cheaters are weak-willed. They can be smart, powerful, wealthy, talented, successful. But these other measures of strength don't matter. Never being able to trust your man is what makes this a Dealbreaker. It will drive you crazy.

Many men believe that cheating is OK, that it is just a "physical" thing and "doesn't mean anything." This is garbage. Everyone, especially The Cheater, knows it is *THE* biggest violation of trust. When someone knows something is wrong, self-control can and should prevent them from doing it—whether it's stealing a car or cheating on a spouse.

Think about it this way: When someone cuts your guy off on the highway, he might feel like killing them. But he doesn't! Do you know why? Because killing people is wrong and he knows it. This goes for all of us—when we know something is very wrong, everyone except the mentally ill knows how to control their behavior.

Cheating can and should be held to that same standard: It's wrong! "But Honey, I couldn't help myself." What a load of crap. He *COULD* have—he just *CHOSE* not to. You can be sure his infidelity will come with lots of excuses. Maybe even with an accusation or two. I will debunk some of The Cheater's favorite excuses later in the Conventional Wisdom section.

## BE SURE YOU REMEMBER THIS...

### It Has Nothing to Do with You

Guys who cheat simply lack the willpower to resist temptation and/or the courage to tell you they are no longer in love with you. These are character flaws which will never go away. A Good Man will do the right thing and not mess around. A Good Man will tell you he needs to leave your relationship if he no longer loves you. Tough? Sure. Correct? Without question. Most times, cheaters cheat and it has nothing to do with you—it's all about them and their egos. Simply put, they are just Losers.

You might look at yourself and wonder if it's you. Is it because you are not attractive enough anymore? Hell no! Brad Pitt cheated on Jennifer Aniston. You know why? He had the opportunity and he lacked the willpower to do the right thing. Tiger Woods? Arnold Schwarzenegger? Losers!

A Good Man will always do the right thing. He can resist temptation. If he is questioning his feelings, as difficult as it might be, he will tell you well before he strays. A Cheater just goes right ahead.

IT ALL COMES BACK TO THE KEY ELEMENTS: Discipline and self-control. Your man either has them or he doesn't. Don't be the poor soul who thinks you can change him. These good characteristics are instilled young and are on display almost every day. The Cheater has neither, and you do not want to waste your time hoping for a miracle.

### The Bottom Line

Cheating should always be deemed a permanent and fatal character flaw. Call him on the carpet and break it off. If there is a bright side, it's that The Cheater is easy to shed in that he will usually go away (and stay away) without a fight. He will quickly move on to the next girl... which he has proven already.

IMPORTANT: If he comes rolling back around, don't let him charm his way back in. Once a Cheater, always a Cheater.

**#3**

# THE ASSHOLE

*"I've found the key to happiness. Stay*
*the hell away from assholes."*
*– Rotten eCards*

Allie was a former Denver Nuggets Dancer. There were guys who would have given their right arm to even have her smile at them. But Allie was not on the market. She was in a committed relationship. She was still dating her college boyfriend, who was a former basketball star. "Star" would be the operative word here. He was a piece of work, strolling into the bar like he owned the place.

He would sprawl out in a booth and demand his cocktail. No "please" just a "yeah, I want." Then his entourage would roll in. I say entourage, not friends, because he treated them like they were privileged just to be hanging out with him. And if they were privileged, then Allie was the luckiest woman in the world to be his girlfriend. He'd even let her buy his drinks. It was unbearable to watch. He was an Asshole.

The most easily recognized of all types of Losers, I am always amazed at how many women like Allie I see on the arm of The Asshole. Part of The Asshole credential revolves around success and power. These are guys who have it and use it to abuse others, like a guy with superpowers choosing to be a supervillain versus a superhero.

This is the guy who treats everyone around him poorly because he can get away with it. He might even be the guy your friends warned you about before you fell for him. Chances are, if your girlfriends hate your boyfriend in spite of his pedigree, he is an Asshole.

Assholes are readily identifiable—you know one when you see one. Hollywood does a great job of portraying Assholes, such as Billy Zane in *Titanic* or Bradley Cooper in *Wedding Crashers*. Often a combo-pack of the bad traits that come in succeeding chapters, The Asshole will initially manifest himself socially. When people begin declining your dinner invitations, stop inviting you out with the group, and seem to cut time together short for the silliest of reasons—and you are certain the problem is not you—then it is your boyfriend. Yep. Asshole.

Also, if you actually call the man you're currently with an Asshole with any degree of frequency, time to kill that relationship off. This guy is just being nice because he wants you. Due to his inherent nature, he'll ultimately mistreat everyone around him—you will be no different.

Here is an additional test: Introduce this guy to the most upbeat, positive person you know. It's important that you like this person and know that he or she universally adores everyone. Have them spend some real time together. Your confirmation will lie in either (a) positive person hates boyfriend, (b) boyfriend hates positive person, or (c) the dislike is mutual and apparent. He is likely an Asshole or, at the very least, a Douchebag (covered later).

## The Bottom Line

Dumping The Asshole is easy. He will be amazed—maybe even indignant—that you are walking away from all that he offers. No worries. His pride will ensure you never hear from him again.

---

## **MOVIE NIGHT HOMEWORK**

Here are some movies featuring world-class Assholes:
*Titanic* (Billy Zane)
*Wedding Crashers* (Bradley Cooper)
*Beauty and the Beast* (Gaston)

---

**Movie characters you're *supposed* to like
who are really nothing but Assholes:**

Robert Downey, Jr. in *Iron Man*
Matt Damon in *Good Will Hunting*

**#4**

# THE ALCOHOLIC (*vs.* THE DRINKER)

*"The idea that somehow, someday*
*he will control and enjoy*
*his drinking is the great obsession*
*of every abnormal drinker.*
*The persistence of this illusion is astonishing."*
*– Alcoholics Anonymous, The Big Book*

When I was in college, I took a survey designed to assess my risk of alcoholism. Given my family history, I took it with a bit of trepidation. It was a rather odd survey for a young guy in a fraternity to take. "Do you usually drink until all the alcohol is gone?" (It's a party, right?) "When sober, have you ever regretted something you've said or done while drinking?" (Haven't we all.) "Have you noticed your tolerance increasing over time?" (Heck yeah!)

I think I answered in the affirmative to just about every question except "Do you drink alone?" and "Do you sometimes hide your drinking?"

The assessment went on to speculate that even a single yes could indicate a problem, while multiple yes's made your alcoholism a virtual certainty. Given the realities of being young and on campus, the survey was pretty much worthless, but at some point in your future, it can become relevant. How do you know when, though? How can you tell the difference between someone who is an Alcoholic and someone who is a Drinker?

This is the fundamental challenge of separating The Drinker from The Alcoholic. It is an awfully tricky one, as well, because so much of socializing and dating revolves around parties, dinners and otherwise going out. Initially, The Drinker and The Alcoholic can both seem like great guys. Both might be.

Either way, The Alcoholic or The Drinker is likely to be a fun guy to party with. The critical thing to deduce is the frequency and control of the drinking. Most guys drink socially. Many occasionally overdo it. So how do you separate the social drinkers—even the binge drinkers—from the guys who have an alcohol problem?

Let's start with control. I believe one of the earliest and most accurate indicators is the ability to *STOP* drinking once you start. If you've been on numerous dates with someone (and you both totally overdid it on *ONE* of those nights), that was probably just the fun carrying you away. But if every one of those dates ends up with your guy slurring words, acting sloppy, or otherwise losing control of himself, then he (and you) probably have a problem. Context is critical. An unexpected party materializes? Understandable. He's blotto at the movies? Not looking good. If the situation calls for partying? Then OK. If it calls for restraint and he blows it every time? Problem.

Similarly, you should try to note if your man can go on a date without drinking... at least significantly. For example, can he truly have just one beer with dinner? Is he able to walk away from a cocktail that still has a sip in it? Can he say "I'm not drinking tonight" and then actually not drink?

Frequency is another telltale sign. Especially when you are young, drinking is often a part of the regular social routine. But it should not slip into the realm of daily... ever. Unless you are on a Spring Break trip or some other protracted outing, drinking more than a day or two in a row should signal the problem. Daily drinking, especially *heavy* daily drinking without reason or occasion, is proof positive of The Alcoholic.

The Alcoholic *ALWAYS* wants to drink, needs to drink. The Drinker can opt out, even when it's hard... even when you expect him not to. This is the crucial distinction. Willpower. An Alcoholic just *IS*, and alcoholism, like family, is with you for life.

Take it from me, the problems this will lead to are deadly serious and too numerous to count. Drunk driving. Job loss. Blackouts. But perhaps the worst is the fact that for The Alcoholic, alcohol comes first. It is Number One. That means the best you can hope for is to be Number Two in The Alcoholic's life.

This book is not about you playing second fiddle to anyone or anything. Playing second fiddle to alcohol is just plain sad. As hard as it may be, and as good a man as The Alcoholic might be, it is best to get out of the relationship early. The heartbreak of living with, and trying to reform, The Alcoholic is well documented and the chances for sustained sobriety are not good. These situations are compounded by the fact that when sober, Alcoholics can be some of the finest, kindest people around.

## The Bottom Line

The line between "OK" and "problem" can be pretty thin. To really test what you're dealing with, create some situations where he can demonstrate some control. If he can't, then you need to get out. If he's consistently choosing drinking over you, then there's a problem. You'll need to stay strong on this, too, as he's very likely to drunk-dial you for many weeks afterwards, if not drunk drop-by.

---

### *KEEP IN MIND...*

A guy who's been drinking may behave
in a way you have never seen
before. This may offer real insight into his true self.

---

## *Related to and tied with #4*

## THE DRUG ADDICT (*vs.* THE DRUG USER)

Ditto the previous alcoholic scenario and just insert the word "drug" for "alcohol." Of course, if it's a heavy drug (crack, meth, heroin), then this is a Dealbreaker for certain. There is no realistic rehab chance.

*"I wasn't even 20 at the time, but it
taught me something about drugs.
They can take a good man, a warm, funny, loving
man, and turn him into a loser and worse."
– Michael Bergin*

**#5**

## JEALOUS & POSSESSIVE GUY

*"A competent and self-confident person is
incapable of jealousy in anything."*
*– Robert Heinlein*

*"I hate possessiveness. I'm nobody's possession."*
*– Olga Kurylenko*

Jack was one of the best guys I had working for me and he seemed to have it all–he was tall, handsome, fun-loving, and hard-working. The guy could even play the saxophone. We spent quite a bit of time together outside the workplace—and, other than some self-confidence issues, he seemed bulletproof. Even better, my whole family liked him. I thought he was a solid guy and a good catch for some lucky gal.

I decided to introduce him to Katie, who was single and, as an occasional babysitter, also a family favorite. They hit it off and quickly got pretty serious. Not exclusive, but seemingly on the way. I thought we'd made a real love connection. Then Jack's insecurities started to show up... in the worst possible way.

Katie was still out in the dating pool, and it quite literally drove Jack mad. He could not deal with it. I would try to coach him through his bouts of insane jealousy, but there was no helping it. He started stalking her. She eventually had to get a restraining order. In spite of all his gifts and all he had going for himself, Jack turned out to be Jealous & Possessive Guy.

A self-explanatory combo of red flags, Jealous and Possessive Guy (JPG) is a big, psychological mess from the moment he decides he digs you. JPGs lack such confidence in themselves that they are probably amazed to have caught your interest in the first place. As flattering as this may sound, you do not want to end up babysitting one of these head-cases. A first and very clear indicator for this guy is the perpetual "I love you." If you can't ever leave his sight or hang up the phone without him searching for reassurance that you still love *him*, then you have earned the attention of a JPG.

At first it might seem charming, the constant seeking of your avowed love, but underlying this is a genuine fear that you will leave him. This is the unhealthy and dangerous part. If he is continually seeking reassurance from you when you are together, he is tearing himself apart with doubt when you are away. The JPG is the type of man whom you will discover reading your emails, or going through your phone, or wondering who that guy he saw you talking with was.

Healthy relationships are built on a foundation of trust, and if he can't trust you when you are apart, then that foundation will never be strong. You want and need a man who has the confidence in himself *AND* you. He needs to be perfectly comfortable with your going out and living your life in a normal, everyday way without ever suspecting you are off flirting with someone else the moment you're out of sight.

Even worse are the JPGs who think you are being unfaithful right in front of their faces. Have you ever been to a party and seen one of these guys come unglued because his girlfriend is talking to another guy *RIGHT IN FRONT OF HIM!?* I mean, WTF? Does he actually think you are picking up on someone while he's in the very same room? It just shows the crazy level of insecurity the JPG carries around with him.

So, take note: The JP Guy is dangerous if combined with The Fighter—and even worse when combined with The Abuser.

## The Bottom Line

JPG can be a difficult Loser to get rid of, but you have to *FIRMLY* explain to him that you no longer love him. Unfortunately, it is highly likely that you may have to do this over and over again. If he continues to pursue you, you may even have to get a restraining order. Do it. The JP Guy hanging around can prove harmful to both you and any future relationships you pursue.

**#6**

# THE LIAR

*"The sad truth is that most of my husbands
turned out to be convincing liars."*
*– Joan Collins*

*"If a man lies to you, he is behaving
badly and unlovingly toward you.
He is disrespecting you and your relationship."*
*– Susan Forward*

Abby loved Kevin. Heck, we all did. He was just that likeable combination of charming, ambitious and outgoing. They had been dating for only a short time, but things had gotten intense very quickly. He moved into her place for practical reasons. Kevin was working on a business plan to open his own restaurant and had raised most of the money. It was already in escrow while the deal was getting finalized. He came to work for us in the meantime to make a few extra bucks. The plan rapidly morphed to include Abby. Now it was *THEIR* plan. It was all the stuff of dreams coming true. It turned out to be total bullshit.

The first indication of trouble began with the lack of money. Abby was picking up the tab for virtually all of the living expenses because Kevin was "coming up with his cash-match" for his investor money. His deal kept getting pushed back because of "legal stuff." Then he got served with a garnishment that "must have been a mistake." Then Abby discovered he had been married before... about the time I figured out he was stealing from the company. He actually tried to explain it all away, in the face of overwhelming evidence to the contrary. He really seemed to believe his own story and, worse, we *WANTED* to believe his story! Kevin was a total Liar.

If the foundation of a good relationship is trust, then The Liar, by definition, is not a suitable mate. The Liar is a smooth talker who effortlessly makes up stories to cover a myriad of behaviors. So it is really just a matter of time before he tries to foist one of the whoppers on you. And thus it begins.

At first blush The Liar also appears to be a pretty self-explanatory personality, but he is not actually so cut-and-dried. All people are prone to telling untruths on occasion, and the "little white lie" should not be mistaken for what The Liar engages in. The Liar is someone who tries to talk his way out of everything versus embracing responsibility. I almost wanted to label The Liar "Mr. Breaks-His-Word-Guy," but that doesn't fully capture some of his behavior.

Typical phrases from The Liar begin with "I never said that," "I didn't know," and "I have no idea what you're talking about." This is often done with a straight face because it is possible you slightly misquoted him, or didn't specifically say no or did not recall a prior conversation verbatim. The bottom line is you *KNOW* that he understood and he is trying to create the wiggle room necessary to shirk the blame.

The poor Liar is very easy to flush out and discard, as bad bullshit is bad bullshit. He may even be lovable, but you can't tolerate this behavior in a relationship.

More insidious is the skilled Liar, the guy who has become so adept at crafting plausible tales that you will want to believe him. He will cling to his story and become indignant, maybe even attempting to swing the blame all the way around to you. It may be impossible to disprove his version of events, but the bottom line is *YOU* know he is not coming clean.

The skilled Liar will never acknowledge wrongdoing unless the evidence is irrefutable... and sometimes not even then. This greatest persuader often falls back to the old tactic of getting angry and then dropping the "you never trust me" line on you. If, in fact, you find yourself never trusting your man, then it will never work out for the two of you, anyway. Actions speak louder than words, so get it over with.

## The Bottom Line

You catch him lying, he is a Liar. The explanation will probably be good. The better it is, the bigger a Liar he is. You need to tune out the explanations and kick him out. The Liar will then move on to the next victim when he realizes you won't be fooled again.

---

**SOMETHING ELSE TO KEEP IN MIND...**
A guy who is keeping a bunch of secrets
is a Loser—probably a Liar,
maybe a Cheater—but a Loser for certain.

---

**#7**

# THE FIGHTER

*"To injure an opponent is to injure
yourself. To control aggression
without inflicting injury is the Art of Peace."*
*— Morihei Ueshiba*

We had just promoted Heather to run our newest bar. I dropped by to check on things and, as I stood at the rail, a drunk guy came rolling up and stood right beside me. I could feel him leaning into my personal space as I talked with Heather. I finally turned to look at him when I realized he wasn't going away. I could feel the hostility. "Can I help you, buddy?"

Turns out he was Heather's boyfriend, Mike. He was young, athletic, easily 20 years my junior... and about half my size. He was also drunk. Introductions were made and things appeared to be fine until I suggested Mike had maybe had enough to drink. I kid you not, he steps back, rips his shirt off and yells, "You want a piece of me?!" I would have started laughing had I not seen a thousand Mikes in my bars over the years. He was dead serious. He had a wild look in his eyes. Mike was a Fighter.

Simply put, The Fighter gets in fights... all the time. It is something he seeks out and can't put away once it's started. The Fighter might be "good" at fighting, or he might get his ass kicked every time. This is not about how tough he might be. It is about the inability to keep himself under control—that is the concern.

Now, most guys want to be brave for their women, and you should always want to have a man around who will defend you to the death... so be careful not to confuse natural, instinctive protectiveness for The Fighter. The Fighter loses his head. The Fighter throws punches first and negotiates later. The Fighter wants to fight with people who do not want to fight with him... including you.

Everyone gets mad on occasion; everyone gets into some sort of a fight here and there. But when identifying The Fighter, it is partially about looking for the frequency of fury and, more importantly, looking for the physical reaction. A normal person can get angry, even furious, but they get it under control and eventually calm down... without violence. The Fighter lacks this coping mechanism. The Fighter just starts lashing out at people, even someone who was not involved at the onset. They can be sorry as heck two seconds later, but this momentary loss of reason is a Dealbreaker.

Volatility like this is never good for a relationship. Not only can guys like this turn their violence on you (always "accidently" by the way), but down the road they could turn their anger loose on your kids. Whether or not you'd be able to forgive him is beside the point. Dating anyone who might hurt you must be an automatic Dealbreaker—just like it is with The Abuser.

Guys like The Fighter are tempting partners because they are emotional, passionate men. They wear their emotions on their sleeve. But without self-control, you are signing up for an eventual date with big problems.

## The Bottom Line

The Fighter is almost certain to get angry when you break things off, so do it in a public place. If you are confident he is not potentially an Abuser, then you won't need to be concerned for your safety, but I'd play it safe. No matter what, you'll want to be aware of The Fighter's whereabouts for the sake of your next boyfriend. There is a good chance he will be itching to take on any guy you're hanging out with in the foreseeable future.

**#8**

## CREEPY GUY

*"Women always try to see the one
good part of the weird guy
because the dating landscape is so bleak.
Women will say, 'He's very odd, but he likes to cook.
He's creepy, but he makes good pancakes!'"
– Zoe Lister-Jones*

A friend of ours got engaged a few years back to a guy that I thought was fairly normal. He had a good job, could hold a conversation... was even a candidate for public office. But something about him set off my wife's radar—she got a weird vibe from him. And she wasn't the only one. Her sister felt it, too. I thought it was their imagination. They both thought he got a "little handsy" with his hugs. "Was that a butt-grab or an accidental hand-brush when he said goodbye?" Come on! He's engaged to our friend—and she was standing right there!

But the girls couldn't shake the feeling that it was deliberate with this guy, that he was definitely creepy. Other women in our group spoke up about him, too. Then, just two months later, my wife busted him holding hands and kissing at the park... with another woman, not his fiancé. Nice. Creepy *AND* a Cheater!

So, if anyone you know and trust ever refers to your man as creepy or drops the old "he gives me the creeps" line, consider that a giant red flag. There is no reason for anyone you date to ever give off a creepy vibe to *ANYONE*. It should make you feel creepy just knowing you're with a guy like that. Let him go ASAP... and hope he's not actually creepy enough to linger.

Another variation of Creepy Guy is Inappropriate Physical Contact Guy, the man who puts the moves on women he meets who have no relationship with him at all. This Creep is the guy who goes in for a goodbye hug with your friend and slips her the tongue. He should set off everybody's alarm systems immediately.

## The Bottom Line

It's tough to tell someone you're breaking it off because he's Creepy, so just use a conventional excuse (see the list later in the book). If he lingers afterwards, or becomes lurky *AND* Creepy, don't hesitate to get a restraining order.

**#9**

# THE BIG TALKER & THE FREELOADER

*"A man is not considered a good man
because he is a good talker."*
*– Gautama Siddhartha, founder of Buddhism*

*"Freeloader: Someone who sits around
and doesn't work and mooches
off their family and steals all their mom's
hard earned money to do nothing
all day and contribute shit to society."*
*– Urban Dictionary*

*"Actions speak louder than words." – Your Dad*

This is the first chapter where I am at a loss to kick things off with a specific story. You know why? Because I have heard so much big-talking from customers, buddies, and co-workers over the years, that I can't even separate out some stories as more relevant than others. We guys like to talk and dream big. Only some of us will go on to try to make things happen. Big talk, versus big action, is so endemic to the male species that we should really arrive with a warning label.

The Big Talker is always full of big plans to better his lot in life. Getting ahead involves hard work. Procrastinating demonstrates an inability to even get started. Quitting after starting is just a tiny bit better than not starting at all. The kind of man you want will just go out and get it done. He will need your encouragement, he might even need a nudge now and then, but he will work in the right direction.

Real men will be, or will *WANT* to be, employed. They will *WANT* to be the breadwinner. Does your man constantly complain about his job but do nothing to change his lot in life? Does he dream big but then do nothing to get there?

The Big Talker is just a mirage. There is no substance behind the talk... and no substance behind the man. The saddest thing about the Big Talker, and something which makes them difficult to spot, is that many of them genuinely come to believe their own bullshit. They are their own biggest fans, and they have often deluded themselves... right along with you. A real work ethic is one of the easiest things in the world to spot—it's *WORKING*, even if it means working to find work!

The Big Talker can also evolve into the even worse condition of The Freeloader. These guys dream so big, they are unwilling to "compromise" their standards to take a job that's beneath them. If you ever meet a charming, able-bodied guy who's unemployed, *WAIT!* See if he finds and holds down a job and *then* consider dating him.

The Freeloader is often quite charming... and is usually a Big Talker, too. My advice is to never date an unemployed man—that way, you guard against falling for one of these con artists. A real man will find a job soon enough, even if it is beneath his skill level—or otherwise be out searching for one. The Freeloader might take a job for a short while, but not for long if you are there to ride to the rescue.

There are loads of guys out there playing on their Xboxes all day while their girlfriends and wives are out working to make ends meet. If you ever find yourself paying the rent and your man has not been out looking for work every single day of that month, then it is time to cut your Freeloader loose. And don't fall for the Big Talk he'll give you when you kick him out. *SURE*, he's close to landing something big. Tell him to come back when it's a done deal!

Letting you pay for everything will bug a Good Man—bug him to the point of making him want to hide and not come back until he can provide for you, or at least contribute. Don't get me wrong, you as a woman, can earn your own way and even be the primary breadwinner... but it should bug him.

Like Kurt Russell in *Overboard*, the kind of man you want will swallow his pride to provide.

(I have promised to put an important qualifier on this last bit, so here it is: *IF* your man is actively working toward his future and you both know it, then of course it is fine for you to support him. He's in med school? That counts. He's actively funding his technology start-up? Sure. You have means and he's a work-study student earning his degree? Yeah, of course, you can buy dinner.)

## The Bottom Line

Because these types of guys are plentiful and not harmful in the typical way, it can be pretty easy to fall into a relationship with one of them. Short term, it is probably even tolerable. But who he really is will become more evident over time. You may grow numb to it, though, so this is a pretty fair place to lean on your friends and family for feedback. If they think you've hooked a Big Talker/Freeloader, then you need to take a step back and assess—is this what you really want?

## #10

## CAREER SINGLE GUY

*(Think Mr. Big from the "Sex and the City" HBO series.)*

Also known as Never Getting Married Guy, this is a man who knows his prospects for meeting and bedding lots of women is good and is only going to get better over time (which is absolutely true as the balance of gender power shifts). Most of these guys are older, they have seen their dating lot in life improve dramatically, and they are planning to ride their perceived good fortune to the end of their days. Career Single Guy (CSG) is usually fun, charming, and successful, so he might appear to be quite the catch. And therein lies the problem... he's not catchable.

Most of my buddies who are CSGs are very happy with their decision, have no desire to change, and have been that way since they graduated from college. Maybe you can hook up with a CSG, and perhaps even have some fun, but you have to move along sooner or later, as this temporary monogamy is only yours for a fleeting period of time.

### The Bottom Line

Just tell him it's over. He is not expecting you to stay with him long-term anyway.

## MORE MOVIE HOMEWORK

Richard Gere plays a CSG in *Pretty Woman*.
Julia Roberts gets her "Fairy Tale" ending
because it's Hollywood. No way would
this ever happen in real life.

# THE NEXT FIVE LOSERS

## *(They missed the first cut, but not by much)*

# SELFISH GUY

*"Selfish persons are incapable of loving others,*
*but they are not capable of loving*
*themselves either." – Erich Fromm*

Ahhh, here we go... Selfish Guy. The guy who has so many important things to do that your relationship kinda gets in the way. This guy is always out doing something... and having a great time doing it. He's golfing. He's at the gym. He's at the ballgame. He's out with the boys. These are all things he loves. Hey girl, you're not asking him to give up the things he loves, are you? How selfish of you!

Wrong! How selfish of *HIM!*

Okay, let's get it out there—all men are selfish. It is in our nature. But it is also something we can overcome... when it is important. *YOU* should be that important. Unfortunately, that is not how Selfish Guy sees things. His hobbies, his friends, his lifestyle are the most important things to him. Asking for some of his time at the expense of his loves is simply unacceptable to him.

Many Selfish Guys end up being career singles (CSGs). It is the reason they never settle down. Much like being Number Two to the alcoholic's liquor, in this case, you are merely Number Two on his priority list of what he enjoys. Do you really want to have your boyfriend make you feel like going out with you is causing him to make a sacrifice? That's garbage. Selfishness is just another form of addiction that can be overcome with discipline and self-control.

And if you think a relationship involves him sacrificing his lifestyle, just wait until he becomes a father. Parenting is the ultimate sacrifice of free time! Taking care of anything you love involves an investment of time... why should you be any different for him? His willingness to give up his time for you should speak volumes, especially after your relationship develops.

---

### *Dad Would Rather...*

You Marry a Thoughtful Guy
than
You Marry a Rich Guy

---

# THE DOUCHEBAG

*"Remember, bring a gift... and no douchebags!" – Scott Schaible*

Similar to The Asshole, The Douchebag is a guy who's a drag to be around... even embarrassing. The difference between the two is The Douchebag's sense of self is way over-inflated, and it's coupled with a total obliviousness of how abrasive he is. Unlike The Asshole, though, he's not mean-spirited. He's just his own special brand of idiot. He'll try to act cool when he thinks people are watching, but of course, everyone sees through the whole routine (eye rolls). But intent does not make for tolerable, so no one will want to be around your Douchebag boyfriend. This is another great instance where your friends will definitely let you know.

Douchebaggery is not only apparent in obnoxious behavior, like overuse of the term "bro," for instance, but also through visual cues and tics (think over-priced sunglasses worn backwards... or at *night*). Hard to excuse—and even harder to put up with. Being a Douchebag isn't a total Dealbreaker (since he's not *trying* to be an unlikable jerk). You can successfully date a Douchebag for a period of time. Just know that you will be putting yourself in social isolation for the duration.

### *THE ULTIMATE TEST*
### Is he an Asshole or a Douchebag?

| ASSHOLE | DOUCHEBAG |
|---|---|
| Acts like he owns the place | Loudly announces he "knows the owner" |
| Unnecessarily tears other people down | Unnecessarily builds himself up |
| Belittles your accomplishments | One-ups your accomplishments |
| Doesn't care | Doesn't notice |
| The staff looks fearful | The staff looks annoyed |
| Is dismissive | Is oblivious |

---

## **MOVIE HOMEWORK AGAIN**

Watch a Vince Vaughn movie. This guy is a specialist at playing The Douchebag, even when his character is *NOT* supposed to be a Douchebag. He is a clinic on what to avoid!

*Swingers* (unbearably Douchey)
*The Break-up*
*Couples Retreat*

---

# **PLAYING THE FIELD GUY**

*"If she's looking for a commitment and you knowingly proceed so you have something to play with for a while, you might be risking a 'Bobbitt' in your future, and you kind of deserve it."*
*– Judy Cole, How to Play the Dating Field*

While generally disclosing his intentions, at least in part, Playing the Field Guy can darn near persuade you that the best thing in the world for your relationship is to always be open to seeing what else is out there. Another of the most charming types, PTFG thinks it's only natural to see other people. Be warned—only proceed if you *HONESTLY* agree! Not surprisingly, he will tell you that you are at the top of his list.

One of the important things to remember about non-committal men is that they are generally pretty honest with you. You women want honesty, and this guy is giving it to you. It might be thinly veneered to make you think he is serious about you, but that is because he does not want to be perceived as being *too* much of a user and, of course, he needs you to at least *think* you are his favorite. This keeps you in line and sticking around, thinking that he may change his mind and choose you.

Indicators your man is a PTFG include the use of terms like "free-spirit," not wanting to get "tied-down," and the classic "can't we just enjoy each other's company." Unless you are looking for your Booty Call Guy and nothing more, leave PTFG alone. If this guy breaks your heart, at least he can honestly say he warned you.

He is also one of the most tempting men to believe that you can change. You are different. You are special. You *WILL* win his heart exclusively. No, forget it. You won't. If you can truly say you are OK with such an open relationship, then you will be fine with PTFG; otherwise, know that these are among the harder guys to change... and they are often very close to being good men, so don't get sucked in.

P.S. This one's very similar to Loser #10, Career Single Guy—as well as to the next one we'll discuss, Non-Committal Guy. Truly, a charming trio.

# NON-COMMITTAL GUY

*"One of the clearest signs of a non-committer is a procession of lovely exes."*
*– Dr. Pam Spurr*

Not to be confused with Career Single Guy or Playing the Field Guy, NCG is the wishy-washy guy who actually likes you enough to stay with you, but is never willing to commit to the relationship. There have been plenty of young women who've worked for me who've been with their boyfriends for three, four, five years (or more) and there are still no signs of wedding bells.

Now, this is all fine and good if *YOU* truly do not want to get hitched, but experience tells me that is rarely the case. So, ask yourself are you sticking with NCG out of fear that you can't find anything better, or is it just the ease of being in a comfortable relationship?

If he's unwilling to talk about marriage, always saying "later" to the subject, that's a strong signal that you've got a hard-core NCG on your hands. Don't try to force him to commit—and don't get pregnant, thinking that will force his hand (surefire backfire). But do get really clear with yourself—is he worth it as-is, or should you move on? Up to you—it's a question of how much time you want to put in on him and if you really want a reluctant male partner who will likely bolt someday.

## *Dad Would Rather...*

You Marry a Disciplined Guy
than
You Marry a Fun Guy

# SNOBBY GUY

At first blush, it's hard to find fault with Snobby Guy because he's successful, well-dressed, eats at the best restaurants, etc., but the problem with this guy is that he has a superiority complex. Snobby Guy can be refined, well educated, even charming—but he looks down his nose at others because he has more means than they do. This is such shallow hogwash.

The worst sort of Snobby Guy is the guy who was raised with a silver spoon in his mouth. His only real claim to superiority is being born into more money than other guys. Snobby Guy is really a variant on The Douchebag, whose qualities derive from his unfounded feelings of superiority. Snobby Guy has never had to work hard for anything in his life. You do *NOT* want to be the next thing to fall into his lap.

Why is he a poor choice as a mate? Because he tends to be self-centered. Because he is self-indulgent. Because you will really just become part of his "stuff." You deserve to be valued, and that is a feeling you're unlikely to get from this guy.

## LESSER LOSER STUFF

### (Tolerable, but still...)

## THE CHAUVINIST

I considered making this trait a Dealbreaker, as it is hard to imagine a woman falling for any man who thinks women are the inferior sex. It's as if some of the men from *Downton Abbey* jumped into a time machine and traveled to the present day. They might call themselves old-fashioned, but they are really just ignorant. That said, I have known a handful of incredibly smart and talented guys who were more mildly afflicted with this malady, and they have ended up being good husbands. Maybe he'll treat you well because he's also chivalrous. Just know you may end up with Lord Grantham. It could be worse, I suppose.

## STRIP CLUB GUY

Unless you are one of those women who likes to go to strip clubs with your man, which makes it fine, then one of the bigger red flags for a Loser is over-frequenting strip clubs. Unlike watching porn here and there or flipping through a *Playboy*, strip clubs cross the line to within a hair's breadth of cheating.

Now, many of my fellow males will try to say this is just entertainment... but it is not. Strip club lovers are usually the type of men who are one opportunity away from infidelity. Having another woman who's practically naked sitting in your lap cannot be justified as OK simply because it's her job and you're paying her. In many ways this makes it even worse.

Think of going to a strip club as structured straying or an opportunity to cheat with some rules... and many of these clubs even let you bend the rules, so beware.

P. S. Let's be truthful here—what woman in her right mind *really* enjoys going to a strip club? She's going to watch a bunch of sexy, half-naked women tantalize her guy—and that's going to make for a nice evening? If this happens to you and you get invited to go, stand your ground and just say no. It's nothing but a set-up for an incredibly humiliating time.

You're worth more than this! Don't try to be the "cool girl," as Gillian Flynn, the author of "Gone Girl" explained so very well.

## **MR. IMPATIENT**

This is the guy who hates to wait for *ANYTHING*. Lines? Mr. Impatient doesn't like lines, even when everyone else is clearly waiting in one. Explanations? Mr. Impatient would rather skip those and just jump to conclusions. He will make you believe that waiting can actually kill a person. The most fun part is watching Mr. Impatient lose his mind when he tries to find a shortcut around waiting... and it backfires, leading to even more waiting. Yeah, you can live with this guy, but remember you won't be taking in any new, popular shows, dining at any "No Reservation" restaurants or benefitting from any thorough explanations very often. And he will probably be irritated on those occasions when you do.

## A.D.D. GUY

If he's got Attention Deficit Disorder, or even a pretty good likeness of A.D.D., know that you will rarely have his undivided attention for long. He will be most identifiable when you need to share something important and he is already in the middle of doing something. He will keep turning back to the game, the phone, *THE DISTRACTION* constantly... even if what you have to say is quite short. Then he will struggle to recall the details a few minutes later. A.D.D. Guy is more bothersome than harmful, but be prepared to be exasperated by his inability to focus. Squirrel alert!

## THE LOUD TALKER

On the plus side, you will usually hear this guy coming before you meet him. The Loud Talker is that annoying sort who wants everyone to overhear his conversation. The folks three tables away will have no choice but to listen in as he talks about the things he's done, the important people he knows, and the places he's been. You will have to hope your Loud Talker is Coachable (see Good Guy chapter) to have any real chance of shutting this down.

## THE SHOW-OFF

Now, all guys are going to show off a little bit around women... that's part of our mating dance. TSO just doesn't know when to stop. On the plus side, showing off is usually a sign of confidence, which is not a bad thing. You just don't want to be perpetually embarrassed or have to drive him to the ER because he's injured himself pulling some attention-getting stunt. Hopefully, your affection will give him all the confidence he needs to knock it off.

The persistence of this behavior, though, means that he always likes to be the center of attention. But hey, shouldn't that be you? At the very least, shouldn't you be the center of *his* attention?

## THE BRAGGART

The occasional tall tale can be expected from just about any man, but The Braggart makes it a perpetual barrage of one-upsmanship. This is also a very easy jumping off point for him to become a full-fledged Douchebag. It's such a powerful indicator of low self-esteem that you have to hope your love and admiration might help him shut the heck up. Your friends, and *HIS*, will thank you for it.

## CHICKS DIG ME GUY

A variant of the Douchebag, this guy thinks he is God's gift to women. While his behavior is usually a flashing sign that he considers himself super-hot, there is the occasional CDM Guy who will put it out there more overtly... say, with his naked-chick-silhouette mud flaps, his "CHKMAGNT" vanity plate, or his Playboy Bunny t-shirt. Classy.

CDM Guy is so convinced of his own irresistibility, that he is really just one opportunity away from becoming a Cheater. These "opportunities" are usually much more rare for him than he would ever let on, but he's full of big-talk when he's busy bragging about his conquests to his buddies—conquests which are likely fictional, by the way.

## CAN'T GET OVER HER GUY

This guy is a very sad sack of a Loser because he might be a really good guy *BUT* his inability to put his last girl behind him renders him damaged goods, instead of a rebound prospect. You can probably make the assumption that he was dumped by her, but if he's bemoaning a breakup that he initiated, then he's just a dumbass. Let's assume that's not the case.

What you want to note here is his attitude towards her. If he would run back to her should she come rolling around again, then this is a Loser trait as far as you're concerned. Now you know you can't trust that he won't dump *YOU* at her whim. Plus, CGOH Guy can get pretty annoying as he constantly runs on and on about his ex. Monitor from a distance if you want, as this could be minor unless it lingers, but don't go all in and then discover you're second fiddle.

I much prefer the guy who is sad for a while but gets it together and mentally moves on. This means he's recognizing that *HE* wouldn't accept her back in the future because she's now broken for *HIM*. If he truly values trustworthiness and loyalty, which are Good Man traits, then he's going to have a hard time honestly taking her back.

---

## MOVIE NIGHT HOMEWORK

Jon Favreau plays a classic CGOH Guy in *Swingers*.

---

## FITNESS DOUBLE-STANDARD GUY

If you meet a guy who's out of shape but then decides to make comments about *YOUR* fitness, then you have fallen for Double-Standard Guy. Feel free to tell him he's being a dick. Maybe he'll learn, but he's probably not the learning type. This hypocrite has now revealed two character flaws—a shallow love for you *AND* a lack of discipline for himself.

## DON'T-DANCE GUY

Here is another minor indicator of Loserdom: the guy that refuses to dance. I have known many of these men over the years, including my own dad, and most of them are pretty good guys. So why does this classification appear in the book? Because you ideally want a man who will truly put your happiness before his own.

Say you like to dance—maybe even *love* to dance. Now, he can either make you happy while he battles his own dance-phobia issues or he can simply refuse. You really want the guy who's willing to knock himself out to make you happy.

This one is clearly *NOT* a Dealbreaker, but it is an indicator. Don't Dance Guy is pretty much no dancing for the rest of your life with the man you love. I think that's at least a significant loss for you... and a weird refusal. The thing is, if you accept this excuse in the beginning of the relationship, know that these guys *DO NOT* change! I have known only one husband over the past 20 years who managed to break his anti-dance stance. Result? His wife loves that he will now join her on the dance floor... and he's a lot more fun at parties, too.

If you are dating a DDG, you need to ask him why he won't dance, knowing it would make you happier. The response should be enlightening. Theoretically, if it will really, really make him unhappy, then the rule of putting your partner's happiness before your own might cause you to let him slide... in theory.

There is a related guy here, who is virtually identical but less excusable, known as Don't Hold Hands Guy. Either one of these traits gets to be a drag in the long run, so think about it.

## ALWAYS SORRY, NEVER LEARN GUY

Everybody can make mistakes, and your guy will be no different. The thing to watch for is the guy who is *always* making mistakes in your relationship. If he's even halfway worthwhile, he will certainly be sorry for his mistakes. What you want to watch out for here is the guy who repeatedly makes the same mistake and either doesn't learn, or *SEEMS* not to learn, to correct it. This character flaw goes to reliability, at the very least. Remember the old cliché—actions speak louder than words, and sooner or later being sorry is just not enough.

## THE SUPER GOOD-LOOKING

While this is the greatest generalization I will make, I can still tell you it is significant enough that you should be aware of it. Super Good-Looking Guys tend to put less effort into relationships. The root of this is attributable to a lifetime of getting girls easily. This ease can translate into not knowing how to work for a relationship—and not feeling like it's necessary. This is especially true if he's a Playing the Field Guy. If that's the case, watch out—you're in for an unpleasant ride and a rough ending. Finding a new girlfriend is easy for SGL Guy and he knows it.

It may be fun at first to be with this guy—what an ego boost for you, right? Well, that starts to fray when his inevitable narcissism starts to show. But hey, how can he be blamed—he's always been gorgeous and fawned over by women, probably starting with his mother. He's used to it; he expects it—and critically for you, he responds to it.

The thing to know here is that it's baked in, it's practically in his DNA. He's the center of attention, no matter where he is. So, where does that leave you—and how do you cope with the other women he so naturally attracts?

---

## AND THE LESS ATTRACTIVE GUY?

When it comes to healthy relationships, should you bypass the eye candy and go for less attractive guys? Maybe, say researchers from UCLA and the University of Tennessee. Their research discovered that women who are more attractive than their husbands have happier marriages.

The study looked at 82 newlyweds and found that in couples where the woman was more attractive, the man was generally more emotionally supportive; whereas, when the *man* was the better-looking spouse, he tended to be *less* supportive of his mate. "When a guy appreciates his woman (and vice versa) and compliments her on her looks, personality and character, they will have a happier marriage," according to the researchers.

---

*Dad Would Rather...*

You Marry a Fit Guy
than
You Marry a Handsome Guy

---

## THE SUPER CHARMING

Everything about the Super Good-Looking applies to the Super Charming... unless his sense of humor is what makes him super charming, which can be a bonus and perhaps a reason for putting up with him if his narcissistic tendencies are in check. You'll have to decide for yourself on this one.

## PUBLIC DISPLAY OF AFFECTION GUY

If he feels the need to make out in public, just ask him to stop. But ask yourself why he's doing this—is it because he's possessive and wants the world to know you are "his"? Or maybe he's just insecure? Whatever the motive, he probably doesn't know this makes you *both* look bad. Holding hands is one thing, but making out is something else entirely. Yuck! So, if he's a PDA Guy, let him know how uncool this is. And then don't put up with it.

## THE WUSSBAG

Your guy does not have to be super-manly, but he should be able stand up for himself. Any guy who can't advocate for himself is going to be an even bigger pushover when he needs to stand up for you as a couple... or a family. Now, you might enjoy bulldogging some situations on your own, but you need your guy to have a spine when it really counts. The Wussbag just rolls over in every situation. This isn't about his willingness to compromise, or about being stubborn—it's about being able to say enough is enough when he needs to. The Wussbag folds to pressure every time. That's just a non-starter. At the very least, he needs to have the courage to stand up for himself to you!

## FLASHY GUY

Closely related to The Show Off, Flashy Guy displays his insecurities via his car, clothing and other possessions. He should really just get a "Low Self-Esteem" tattoo across his forehead.

## MR. SECRETIVE GUY

If you didn't know better, you would think this guy worked for the Secret Service. Nothing is revealed easily with this character. Every conversation can feel like an interrogation with an uncooperative suspect. If you get a few months in with your new man and you still know virtually nothing about him, he is probably Mr. Secretive Guy. He is a tough one to assess.

At best, he has some things he wants to keep private. At worst, he's hiding a whole bunch of Dealbreakers. Everybody has the right to keep some personal things private, but transparency becomes increasingly important as a relationship progresses. This guy will need to start trusting you and open up over time or you will start distrusting *him*. And you probably should.

---

### *Dad Would Rather...*

You Become a Crazy Cat Lady
than
You Marry a Loser

---

## A WORD ABOUT BAD BOYS

Many women find themselves attracted to Bad Boy types. Surprisingly, this is fine if it doesn't apply to his relationship with you. The key character flaws you are watching for don't have much to do with being a Bad Boy. If he has a good heart, treats you well, and avoids most of the stuff I've listed previously, then love away. He might be a troublemaker, but as long as he's not a troublemaker for *you*, things are fine.

## Ten Opening Lines to Help You Dump Him

1. It's not you, it's me. *(a tried and true classic)*

2. I can't do this anymore...

3. It's not fair to you that I'm not in love with you.

4. I've met someone else I'd like to see. (whether you have or not)

5. You're an asshole. *(just for Assholes)*

6. You broke my heart and I will never get past that.

7. Somewhere along the way I just fell out of love with you.

8. Our relationship is broken and it's best for us both to move on.

9. I really need someone who places my happiness first.

10. I will never look at you the same way, and that's not fair to either of us.

### *One Last Reminder...*
### MEN DON'T CHANGE...*Especially Losers*

Men are creatures of habit. They just don't change unless they *have* to, and that's usually only when the stakes are really, really high. And even then, it takes a supreme act of will on their part—which will likely be unsustainable. So, keep this in mind if you have a partner with any of the flaws we've just discussed.

Obviously, some of the Dealbreakers (Cheating, Abuse), should not even be given the opportunity for change. Period. Ever. End of story. What you need to think long and hard about are the others.

Most of the Losers on the list have traits that will erode your relationship over time—and these guys are very unlikely to change. Can you live with that? Do you want to? Probably not. If he really likes you, yet the behavior persists, you should pull the ripcord.

That is why this list is so important. You need to know what you're up against. And face it—if you decide to stick with him, your Loser's problems are probably with you forever.

**The TV show *The Office* is full
of Loser guy examples:**

Michael Scott – Douchebag
Dwight – Chauvinist
Jim – The Good Man
Ryan – Big Talker
Creed – Creepy
Andy "The Berndog" – Snobby Guy
Toby – Wussbag
Kevin – Fitness Double-Standard Guy
Stanley – Cheater
Robert California – Asshole

## *A Special Case:*

## <u>UNAWARE HE'S GAY GUY</u>

*"At least 5 percent of American men, I estimate,
are predominantly attracted to men,
and millions of gay men still live, to
some degree, in the closet.
The evidence also suggests that a large number
of gay men are married to women."*
*– Seth Stephens-Davidowitz, the New York Times*

We got the note along with several other family friends. Tom and Sarah were getting divorced after three kids and ten years of marriage. They wanted to let those closest to them know before the news broke widely. We were surprised, as they had stuck together through some tough times, including the recession and loss of a business. The reason for the divorce? Tom had finally come to terms with something he had known since before he met Sarah–he was gay.

Most women have pretty good gaydar... but some don't. And most gay guys know whether they're gay—even if they can't admit it to the outside world (or sometimes even to themselves). But here's the tricky part—many of these guys appear to be perfectly straight, *GREAT* guys—especially in the cases where they have not yet come to terms with their sexuality. This can lead to protracted male-female relationships—and even marriage, which will later, inevitably end in heartbreak.

Curiously, the Unaware He's Gay Guy is most often accurately spotted by other men. If you have any suspicions about your guy, and another man you trust should let fly with the comment "that guy seems gay" or "I thought he was gay," then maybe he is. I can think of a half-dozen guys I know like this right now... and four of them are, or have been, married! It happens more often than you would think, especially when they check all of the Good Man boxes. I think it is prevalent enough that you need to at least be aware that UHG Guy is out there... and dating women (for now).

Remember, he's not a Loser as a human being, in fact he might end up being your best friend, but UHG guy is definitely not your future husband either.

A very straightforward way to assess your guy's UHG possibilities is to have a frank discussion about each of your sexual histories. If he has any homosexual experimenting in his past, then this has to raise a red flag. Multiple experiences would clearly indicate he's in denial of his true nature. If you care about each other, this should be a fair topic to broach. You will have to judge his honesty for yourself.

In the absence of this type of clarity, you'll have to just be a keen observer. Many of the UHG Guys I know have inadvertently outed themselves when out drinking. Sometimes a couple of cocktails loosen up the inhibitions and, *POW*, suddenly the guy with the girlfriend is getting pretty cozy with another man. I think this is compounded by the drunken tendency to think you are being discrete, too. While alcohol is no helper if your man is The Alcoholic, it very well might save you from a big mistake if it reveals the true sexual preference of a UHG Guy you've fallen in love with.

## The Bottom Line

You have to end this relationship but it may not be easy. He's in denial, after all. The UHG men I know who have come out have all acknowledged that, to some degree, they always knew they were gay. I think you have to count on this resonating with your UHG Guy on some level when you let him go.

# Part II

# CONVENTIONAL WISDOM
## Dad's True-False Test

### "A Good Man Is Hard to Find"
### Dad's Judgment: TRUE

If you first consider that you need to be attracted to a guy and then need to discover you have good chemistry, the math is already not working in your favor. Couple this with the statistics on the Losers I have just outlined—Abusers and Cheaters alone knock a big chunk out of the eligible bachelor pool—and you can see that the Good Man is quite a rarity. It might seem disheartening, but remember this—you are quite a catch yourself and you are worth it!

### "Good Things Come to Those Who Wait"
### Dad's Judgment: FALSE

While this is not an argument for rushing into things, in the case of women and relationships, it is just a sad fact that those who wait too long often miss the boat on Mr. Right. When Good Guys go off the market, they rarely come back on it. The pool only gets more shallow as you get into your 30s and beyond.

You are young and in the prime time of your life for socializing and meeting guys right now, so get out there and (carefully and reasonably) go for it! Meet lots of people, have lots of experiences. Be social. Be fun. That's how you are going to unearth the Good Guys— and then settle on the right guy. Don't sit back and assume you can get around to looking later. That's how you end up being Crazy Cat Lady... which, tragically, is still better than ending up with a Loser.

### "**Breaking up Is Hard to Do**"
### Dad's Judgment: TRUE

There is probably nothing harder than deciding to break up with someone. That said, it will never get any easier, so you owe it to yourself *and* him to get it over with. Now's the time to remember Rule #5: Be decisive and then be strong. Stick to your decision.

### "**Unconditional Love**"
### Dad's Judgment: FALSE

This is a concept created by relationship coaches and religious institutions to keep people pacified. It is a bunch of crap. Love is always conditional... and it should be. If he can't meet the most basic of your conditions, then he is not worth your love. Period. Nothing unconditional about that.

### "**Men Have One-track Minds**"
### Dad's Judgment: TRUE

We are hardwired to think about sex. We like sports and beer, too, but they are distant seconds.

### "**Give Him a Taste of His Own Medicine**"
### Dad's Judgment: FALSE

You are certain your man is cheating on you, so you are considering taking revenge by sleeping with someone else yourself? Bad idea. Years ago I was bartending and had a beautiful woman come to the bar and order a shot. Soon after, she ordered another one. When I asked her why, she said, "I just found out my boyfriend is up in Vail with another woman." Her plan? She was going to get good and drunk and then go home with a random guy from the bar... to get even. Terrible plan. I sat her down and told her, "You know who's going to feel shitty tomorrow? You!"

The idea that your cheating man is going to be punished by your sleeping with someone else is a joke. Why would he care? He is *ALREADY* sleeping with someone else! Maybe, just maybe, his ego would be bruised, but really this form of revenge does not do anything but make him feel OK about what he has done. The best way to get revenge in a situation like this would be for him to come back to town to find his stuff in a box on your front porch. Go, "Beyonce" on that Loser! "Everything you own in the box to the left."

### "__Everyone Deserves a Second Chance__"
### Dad's Judgment: SITUATIONAL

If your man is dropping this line on you, then I would say he probably doesn't deserve a second chance. If it's your mom or your best friend suggesting he might be worthy, then think about it. If the transgression was a Dealbreaker? No way, regardless.

## "Actions Speak Louder Than Words"
## Dad's Judgment: TRUE

This is one axiom you can take to the bank. A Good Man will have his values written all over everything he does. He doesn't just talk about how much he loves you, he *shows* you. Talk is cheap. It's what a man actually *does* that matters. Watch out for it—the Loser is good at making excuses or assigning blame.

> *"Your beliefs don't make you a better*
> *person, your behavior does."*
> *— Sukhraj S. Dhillon*

## "Why Buy the Cow If the Milk Is Free?"
## Dad's Judgment: TRUE

> *"If you're giving a man sex, affection, love,*
> *etc. etc.—essentially giving away*
> *the milk, the cow and the whole damn*
> *farm for free, then he will date you...*
> *without any thought or plan to commit*
> *to you, let alone marry you."*
> *– Wisdom Is Misery, SingleBlackMale.org*

This favorite comes courtesy of *MY* dad. What he told me thirty years ago still holds true today—maybe more so, given the casual, non-committal nature of relationships these days. Needless to say, this is how you could end up with Non-Committal Guy... five years down the road.

### "Father Knows Best"
### Dad's Judgment: OF COURSE

I wrote this whole thing—and every father on the planet will back me up—just ask yours!

### "Play Hard to Get"
### Dad's Judgment: FALSE

One of the great debates in my time behind the bar was the attraction, for men, of the chase. I can tell you, unequivocally, that only wolves like to chase. Acting disinterested and making him go through the brain damage of figuring out your intentions—whether you might be interested in him or not—is maddening for a guy. It's hard enough for a guy to get up the nerve to make the first move, so don't play hard to get unless you really are—and you want him to leave you alone.

Now, this is not a green light to just jump into bed with him. That would be waaay stupid. But you can certainly show interest from the get-go. That's how chemistry works. Don't be too doe-eyed, but if you're attracted to a guy and you have run him through the filter of this handbook, then he's probably worth going out with... minus the silly little chase game.

### *"**A man who marries his mistress leaves a vacancy in that position.**"*
### *– Oscar Wilde*
### Dad's Judgment: TRUE

Sometimes you bring heartbreak on yourself. I never have any sympathy for the woman who falls in love with a married man. By definition, if you find yourself in this circumstance, you are *WITH A LOSER!* Now, if he is divorced, fine, but I am talking about the woman who is sleeping with a married man. This guy will not only break your heart, he will probably never even leave his wife. Even if he does, you are hitching your wagon to a proven Loser. How long after you become his flavor of the week will he be out shopping again? Not long. A guy who cheats on someone, even a girlfriend, to be with you *WILL EVENTUALLY BE CHEATING ON YOU.* This is as close to a guarantee as there is in the relationship world. Get away now!


### "**Familiarity Breeds Contempt**"
### Dad's Judgment: FALSE

When you meet Mr. Right, nothing could be further from the truth. The more you get to know a Good Man, the more you will love him—and vice versa.

### "Past Results Are Not Indicative of Future Performance"
### Dad's Judgment: FALSE

I will lay my bets that past results will pretty much always predict the behavior of any given man. If there is some reason for a serious transgression in the past, then this might mitigate judgment, but if you bring home a guy with a troubled past, you can bet your dad will be on high alert.

### "If It Ain't Broke, Don't Fix It"
### Dad's Judgment: TRUE

If you find a Good Man, don't try too hard to make him better. Let him have a few little imperfections, especially if they make him happy.

### "There's No Better Time than the Present"
### Dad's Judgment: TRUE

Today is the day to get things done. If you're looking for a guy, make some plans to get yourself out there (in person, *NOT* online). If you have postponed breaking things off with a Loser, time to get it done.

### "**Let Me Make It Up to You**"
*(Especially by buying you something)*
**Dad's Judgment: FALSE**

Listen to the song "What You Say" by Jason Derulo. This song typifies everything that a Cheater believes. It is the most ridiculous excuse and half-assed attempt to make things right that I have ever heard. In the song, he's basically acknowledging he was overcome by lust, didn't know what to do when he got found out, and now wants another chance to treat his woman better. I especially like the way he touts her chance to be rich with him when he becomes a star. Wow! What a great deal for her! No apology... just a great opportunity to "live large".

Guess what? He had this woman's love and trust the first time around. He blew it. He "didn't know what to do"? Really?! And now he's going to buy himself another chance? He is going to treat her better this time? Not a chance! I especially love the notion of buying her stuff. Your love should never be purchased, or repurchased. This typifies the disconnect most Cheaters have between what you want and what they *THINK* you want. Losers!

### "**Birds of a Feather Flock Together**"
**Dad's Judgment: TRUE**

Good Men, because of their high personal standards, usually hang around other guys with similar values. If you and your girlfriends can start hanging with a group of Good Men, that will be the finest network you will ever build—a gold mine of men with like values.

And yes, Losers gravitate to Losers. Run! Escape!

## **"The Devil Made Me Do It" or "God Willing"**
### **Dad's Judgment: FALSE**

In my experience, being devoutly religious has absolutely *ZERO* effect on a man's ability to stay faithful. Religious men cheat just as often as secular guys do. The difference is that they often utilize their religion to justify their behavior. How many times have you heard these ready-made excuses? "The Devil made me do it." "I gave in to temptation." "My flesh was weak." Should these excuses really be more powerful than the vow your man has given? Is this the standard to which you think God holds the faithful? Of course not.

That is why adultery is prohibited by the Ten Commandments. It is hugely destructive to individuals and families, and being unfaithful is the highest and worst sort of betrayal. Each person has to deal with it in her own way, but I urge you not to fall into the classic religious trap of turning the other cheek. Think it through and do what's right for you—just know this... you can take the high road and forgive your man his transgressions, but don't fool yourself into thinking that he is anything but a Cheater.

# HERE'S MY PERSONAL FAVORITE...

### "<u>Men Have Needs</u>"
### Dad's Judgment: FALSE

Ironically, this trite saying gives The Cheater the perfect excuse to both justify his behavior *AND* blame it on you. Of course, it's *your* fault! If you had just slept with him more often, he wouldn't have strayed. Oh, BS. Now I am not suggesting you should sexually starve your man to prove his fidelity, but the rule of self-control clearly applies in this situation. Men *WANT* sex. We don't *NEED* it. It amazes me, but I hear this tripe *ALL* the time... "Men have needs." Men say it and largely believe it. Even many women have been brought up to believe this line of reasoning. It is absolutely not true, and here's why—men have been granted two very powerful tools to provide for their own needs: great imaginations and the ability to service themselves.

I jokingly refer to this powerful combination as "ManVision." Men are mentally recording just about every woman they see throughout the day, including *you*, on a DVR in their brain, and men have almost unlimited creativity in editing and recombining these images. So, realistically, need satisfied—itch scratched.

Now, it is not surprising that many men will tell you this is not the same (rationalization), or the Good Book will tell you it is wrong to jerk off, or that your girlfriends will tell you they sleep with their man and he doesn't stray (they are in a happy relationship). If your man loves you and is still attracted to you, he will make every effort to sleep with you—and *only* you.

## "<u>Your Man Has the Right to Expect Reciprocity</u>"
## Dad's Judgment: TRUE

While "men have needs" is a fallacy, this does not mean any guy who loves you should be expected to live in a sexual desert. If you are never in the mood for sex, and he is making a real effort to be with you, then you are being a shitty partner. Reward your man when he makes the effort. It will turn into a reward for you, too.

The most flattering thing for you as a woman should be that your man wants to make love to you. We get it that you are sometimes tired (so are we at times). We get it that you sometimes aren't in the mood, but you can change that if you want to. Turn off the day, your phone, your work, whatever the distractions are—and concentrate on him, on the two of you. Be sexy, be fun, be in the moment. Live now! This is part of what life's all about.

On the other hand, if you find that you are never in the mood, if you never want to make love, then you are simply in the wrong relationship. Sex is a two-way street, and if you are never together *BUT HE IS TRYING*, then you need to reassess your own feelings toward your guy. The bottom line is—if you do not want to make the effort to be with him sexually, then he will (correctly or not) infer that you are no longer into him. Whether that's true or not, you are now in a bed of your own making.

# Part III

# SOME POINTERS FOR MEETING GUYS

## Talking to Girls Is Hard—Asking Girls out Is Even Harder

I think women are often mystified when they know a man is interested in them, but he can't seem to ask them out. This is often compounded by women acting disinterested because they think men love the chase. Let me tell you, getting up the courage to approach a girl you've never met is hard. Some guys manage to make it *LOOK* easy, but it is hard—even for them.

Fear of rejection is not an easy thing to overcome, so sometimes it's just easier to avoid the possibility altogether. Keep this in mind whenever a guy has the nerve to walk up and break the ice. Unless he says something really outrageous (see bad Pick-up Lines below) or he's falling down drunk, try to at least be receptive. If he's not your cup of tea, let him down easy. And of course, if there's a spark there, then feel free to show interest.

Once his nerves are steadied and he realizes you're not going to embarrass him, you'll get a better read on the guy. Another thing—try to never be abrupt with a guy who is sincerely trying to show interest in you. "Get lost" is mean. It's so much nicer to just say "No thanks" or "I'm waiting for someone" to the guy.

I think the nature of walking up and breaking the ice is so difficult for most men that it explains the proliferation of internet dating. They can ask without the face-to-face prospect of rejection, so the impersonal ask is easier. They gravitate here, so you have to, as well.

---

***ALWAYS REMEMBER...***
Let the guy who approaches you down
easy. There is nothing harder
for a guy than getting up the
courage to break the ice!

---

## Pick-up lines

Considering most men do not even use them, the pick-up line is probably the most over analyzed element of the dating scene. While people may debate the efficacy of the pick-up line, one thing holds true: the content of a pick-up line is a pretty reliable indicator of what type of guy has approached you. If it is not awkwardly delivered, guys who use lines, tend to be either Super Charming Guy (Mild Loser) or Sense of Humor Guy (possibly a Good Man).

A great pick-up line can and should indicate interest and sense of humor, all in one non-offensive, door-opening sentence. It can be an amazing icebreaker. A poor, offensive, or cheesy pick-up line swings things the other way. It can instantly indicate a guy is a bit of a Douchebag, a bit taken with himself, or flat-out obnoxious. And that's the thing about pick-up lines—they are either perfect or they are a complete failure. You know it when you hear it, but I will try to illustrate:

Great one: "Do you believe in love at first sight, or should I walk by again?"

Good one: "If I told you 'you have an amazing body' would you hold it against me?"

Bad one: "You must be tired... from running through my mind all night."

WTF?! line: "Did you sit in some sugar? Because you've got a real sweet ass."

Like I said, you'll know it when you hear it!

## **Online and Mobile App Dating**

I know social networking is a modern-day reality, but going off on your own means you are entering a time of your life where you will have virtually unlimited, face-to-face social opportunities. In college there is something going on every hour of the day, every day. This continues for a handful of years after college when everyone is still single. I would highly recommend you take advantage of all the live and in-person activities you possibly can. Save the technology for Googling details on your guy *AFTER* you've met him.

Especially beware of apps like Tinder. They are a guy's dream—these apps are for hooking up. While they might seem harmless at face value, I think they are too much like shopping for the cutest girl you can find at the moment. Hard to imagine things getting more shallow, and I'll bet dollars to doughnuts, this gets used by people only when they are good and drunk. A recent conversation with a sophomore we know at Harvard confirmed this when he likened it to "Snapchat for sex." Don't go here!

---

### *BUT REMEMBER THIS...*

You get out of a process what you put in.
Online and app dating are easy. Meeting people in real life is hard.
Finding the right guy is worth the extra effort,
*SO GET OUT THERE!*

---

## Network through Your Friends' Boyfriends

*"You may depend upon it that he is a good man whose intimate friends are all good..."*
*– Johann Kaspar Lavater*

Obviously, your friends will already be on the lookout for Good Men. But don't forget your friends' boyfriends. If he's a Good Man, then odds are he has some buddies that are also good. When I look back today on the best guys I knew in college (and even high school), there is a common theme—they all had the values of Good Men. And what is more, virtually all of these guys remain true to their character to this day (Men Do Not Change).

Also important, a Good Boyfriend will tell you when you *DON'T* want to date one of his friends. Male friends are the absolute best judges of other men. A question that I have heard asked over and over of men throughout my network is, "Don't you know some single guys? Do you know a Good Man for me?" Women do not realize these categories are not synonymous. With full awareness, the guy (including honest men you know) will always answer, "Not really." This is so telling. They *do* know some single men—they're just all Losers.

---

## Online Dating Tip

Don't insist on a guy whose interests align perfectly with your own. You will limit your matches, and this notion is vastly overrated. You may need to have some things in common, but you absolutely do *NOT* need everything in common.
Trust me when I tell you that it is great to have different interests. You will both want some "me" time in the future when your new-love glow wears off!

---

## Join Some Co-ed Groups

Any co-ed groups where you can be yourself and have fun are ideal places to safely meet someone. I think sport and social leagues are just about perfect—you gather a lot of info on the guys and the events all happen in a pretty low-pressure way. You can learn an incredible amount about a guy just by watching him bowl... or play kickball... or Bananagrams.

Organized outings are similar, less the competitive insights. A day at the zoo or the museum is a great way to observe someone you're interested in without the fog of drinking. Ditto events like festivals and fundraisers. Always try to find the time to go to these things.

### **Volunteer for a Cause**

Some of the finest people in the world are volunteers. What a great place to network. You can find Good Men while showing them you are also a generous soul yourself. And even if you don't meet a great guy, you are placing yourself, in the most positive way, in the networks of Good People who like helping others. They will be on the lookout for Good Men for you, as well.

Where you volunteer is also important. If you love the outdoors, go help clean up some hiking trails. You are certain to find some men there who also love the outdoors. The same can be said for just about any charitable endeavor.

## Absolute Non-factors in Loser *vs.* Good Guy

Income
Education
Profession
Religion *(or lack thereof)*
Intelligence
Race
Hometown

# Part IV

# SOME PERSONAL POINTERS

## Putting Your Best Self Forward

There are plenty of advice books out there that will coach you on how to be all the things a man wants you to be, so I have no plans to tell you how to be more confident, more alluring or more personable. What I will share with you is the knowledge that college represents one of the very rare opportunities in your life when you can re-state who you want to be... even completely reinvent yourself. This is not to say you should try to be something you're not, or that you should pretend to be someone else. What I mean by this is that you are entering an environment where few (to zero) people know anything about you. This means you've got new, multiple chances to make lots of first impressions.

You can consciously strive to become a better woman and a happier one in an environment where you have a clean slate. There are no preconceived notions—so go for it. If you always wished to be a little more outgoing, now's your chance. If your cool side held you back from doing something geeky, guess what? Geek out. If you were always a bit too shy to sing outside the shower, this is your *Glee* moment. Had a bit of an Ice Woman reputation? Banish that to your high school reunions down the road. Take advantage of this chance. You can be a better, happier you... and guys love better, happier women.

---

### *ALWAYS KEEP THIS IN MIND...*
You will draw to yourself the type
of person you want to be.
So go ahead, and be the woman you most
admire, the one you aspire to be.
By being your highest and best self, you
will attract the same in others.

---

## If You See a Guy You'd Like to Meet...

Smile at him. So simple. A woman's smile is worth a thousand words and it lets him know in that one split second that you're approachable.

## *DON'T* Sleep with Him on the First Date!

Much like guarding your reputation, don't assume because he wants to sleep with you that he is "into you." He might not even find you attractive. This is because men have a big, flexible range in between "attractive" and "not attractive" that's called "do-able." Men will sleep with any woman who meets this basic threshold. If you sleep with a guy on the first date because you're sure the attraction is mutual, and then he never calls you again, chances are you fit this category for him. Yes, I know, it further enhances the "men are dogs" theme—and it should, but again... it's just the way it is.

---

### *REMEMBER THIS...*

A guy may pretend to like you just
so he can sleep with you.
I am not aware of a single instance
*EVER* where a woman pretended
to like a guy just to sleep with him.

---

## You Only Have One Reputation

Take care of your reputation. Just like in high school, it is better to be known as a prude than a party girl. This will hold true for your whole life. Be fun, just don't feel the need to be the life of the party. And be careful about hook-ups. I know all about these from the bar business. Hooking up might be fun, but only the woman—not the guy—gets branded with the "Easy A" reputation. Unfair? Yeah. But that's the way it is... and always has been.

### ANOTHER ONE TO KEEP IN MIND...

A guy will pretty much *ALWAYS* sleep
with you if you are willing.
He may or may not like you.

### AND ANOTHER COUPLE OF POINTS...

Yes, sleeping with him on the first
date makes you "easy."
He wants you to drink so you become easier.

## Part V

# SOME ADVICE ON VENUES
## *(Bad, Better & Best)*

### *But first, an important qualifier...*
### <u>BEWARE OF MEN DRINKING IN GROUPS</u>

Before I move on to talk about places, I have to throw out a blanket warning about men drinking in group settings, because they almost always behave worse than men do on their own... or men who are not drinking. This is because men's behavior in groups often gets lowered twice. First, to the standards of the group alpha-male (or males) and then a second time due to the effects of alcohol. It's a bad combination of peer pressure and the desire to conform—and an anesthetized brain.

If you are interested in someone you've met under these conditions, try to meet him one-on-one another time. The drunk, group setting just brings out the worst in most guys, so you will not be able to tell if he's exhibiting pack mentality or his true feelings. Guys in this situation are *NEVER* looking (at that moment) to meet someone for a serious relationship. They are *ALWAYS* just looking to score.

I once overheard a group of men at a downtown bar likening some drunk women across the room to wounded seals. It was an apt and (to them) funny analogy for the many incapacitated women in the room. Clearly, the men were the orca pack. Anyone who watches the Discovery Channel gets the gist of the pack's objective—separate the wounded seal from the group. Mean, low-down, despicable? Yes to all. But this is how male pack mentality operates. It's merciless.

You do *not* want to be the wounded seal. Nor do you want it to be your friend. No one should wake up in a strange bed wondering where she is. Commit, among yourselves, to never let it happen to you.

---

No, you can't get drunk at a party or a bar like a guy can—not without compromising your safety. Never forget this!

---

# PARTY TIME

## Bad

## Fraternity and Other "Man-Group" Parties

While campus parties are almost always the social highlight of any given week, they are also an unsupervised, uninhibited and potentially dangerous place to connect with men. The problem lies in the dangerous combination of Men Drinking in Groups— alcohol, plus opportunity. While you can and will have an amazing time dancing and drinking and flirting at these parties, you must exercise some very deliberate restraint and always ensure that you stay with *your* group.

I'll give you an example of how things can go wrong, big time. When I was in college, there was a fraternity that was known to encourage their pledges to bring drunk women back to their rooms and then have sex with them with the lights on and the window blinds pulled up... *while the upperclassmen sat on a hill outside and watched.* If this had happened in today's connected world, those assaults would likely have gone on to live forever on YouTube.

I tell you this horrible story because I want you to realize that this kind of predatory behavior is still out there—it is still happening today... in fraternities and campuses all over the country.

So, here are a couple suggestions: number one is to meter your drinking. Whether by nursing your beer or watering down your cocktails, do not let your buzz transition into loss of control. As a bartender, I can tell you flat out—do not do shots. Ever! Men love to goad the best drinker among a female group of girlfriends to "show what she's made of." It's "Come on, let's see you do a shot!" This is a trap. You *WILL* lose this contest. The objective is to incapacitate you!

Number two, *NEVER* accept a drink that you did not watch being made or you did not pour yourself. This is not being "bitchy," it is just plain smart. Don't be afraid to discard drinks that are made too strongly. If you don't want to throw them away directly, just set them down discretely and wander away. It might even be telling to see how the men who fed you that drink begin to behave when they (mistakenly) think you have consumed the whole thing.

Sticking with beer is always a good strategy. Beer tends to fill you up and it's lower in alcohol content by volume, so it's harder to get drunk on beer without the warning sign of feeling full. Again, the key is to have fun and be part of the group without losing control of your reason. All of the girls in your group (aka – your Wingwomen) should monitor each other for drunk behavior and any signs of over-consumption.

If anyone is starting to get too out of control or showing signs of visible intoxication, then *IMMEDIATELY* get them out of the party and home safely. Do not just put them somewhere nearby that seems safe (like a bedroom in the fraternity or in the apartment where the party is). Also, do not ask someone else to keep an eye on them. Get them out and see that they get all the way home!

It might seem inconvenient or like it's taking you out of the moment, but this is the most important safeguard you all can guarantee for one another—*ALWAYS COVER YOUR WINGWOMAN!!* Everyone else can return to the party later. It's quite likely no one will even know you sneaked away. If any of the guys question what you're doing, you can consider your dad's suspicions confirmed.

The critical takeaway here is you need to keep one another safe, especially if someone is becoming drunk and can't think straight. Never assume. Err on the side of caution. Trust me, the aftermath of date rape is awful.

All men at parties are not always looking for drunk girls to pull out of the fray, but the bad ones *always* are. That is a certainty, not a supposition. However, if you strictly adhere to the above advice, campus parties can be great fun. You may even meet a guy you want to follow-up with later. The key word being *LATER*. Parties are a good place to network, but not a good place to get to know one another better... and certainly not an appropriate place to hook up.

It's not fair, but your reputation can
be damaged. His cannot.
Have you ever heard of a guy being labeled "easy"?

### Better

### Co-ed or Group-Planned Party

Whether dorm, work or school, any party that is not controlled by a group of men is going to be much safer and probably not as wild as a fraternity party. If the lay of the land is neutral for everyone attending, the odds of anyone trying to make off with a member of your group are much lower. Still, getting any incapacitated Wingwomen home and safe still applies here.

### Best

### You Host the Party

This is the best because you control everything about the venue—what's served, what's allowed, and who can attend. Still, the No Shots rule should remain firmly in place, even on your home turf.

# NIGHT OUT

## Bad: Part I

### Nightclub

Take my Party Time advice and multiply it by ten. Nightclubs are a free-for-all atmosphere with plenty of drinking. The crowd includes randoms from all over town... or, worse yet, visiting from out of town. Bottle service can easily lead to over-service... while you're hanging out on a couch with some big spender you just met. No food service makes intoxication much more likely. If you go, go to just dance with your friends. Clubs are too loud to really meet anyone, anyway. Under no circumstances does anyone get to go home with someone they met here!

I suppose, on the plus side, you will know if you've met Don't-Dance Guy...

## Bad: Part II

### Downtown Bar

You still have the randoms, but at least now you can hear them speak. This may or may not be an improvement. You should also be able to eat something, which you better do! The random-person element is still huge, and many of the men are just out for a good time and trying to score. If you meet someone you're interested in, exchange numbers and follow up for a proper date—but no leaving with anyone *EVER*. Resist any suggestion in your group to fire up Tinder and be sure to count heads before you roll.

## Better

### Neighborhood Bar

Yeah, I'm probably biased but, even though you still have alcohol flowing, the neighborhood bar at least limits the crowd to a more local crew and keeps the volume at a reasonable level. The lack of the random element really makes things safer, as regulars rarely misbehave in the places they frequent. In this type of bar, games provide some competitive fun, and local bartenders are normally engaged enough to cut you off and send you home in a cab, if it comes to that. The main thing is that everyone still goes home together. Something else—I know I've said it before, but be sure to eat something (assuming the kitchen is open), or better still—eat *before* you go out.

---

### *REMINDER...*

Never leave your Wingwoman!

---

# Best

## Casual Restaurant

Think big-group table plus sharable food. Mexican or sushi fit the bill for fun eating choices. This is a pretty safe environment to let another group join you, and the tolerance for any bad behavior will be very limited. Perfect situation.

# SPRING BREAK

### Bad

### Hitting the Beach

Google "Girls Gone Wild." Learn your lesson from those girls. Nothing to do here but drink, get sunburned, and make poor decisions. These shindigs are like fraternity parties without the exclusive access (lots of strangers here). And they're coupled with a swimsuit theme. Perfect situation for all the guys you're trying to avoid. There will be lots and lots of Losers in attendance, including Creepy Guy. Bad news. Double super bad news. By the way, if you go, Dad is *not* paying.

### Better

### Ski Trip

More law and order, more physical activity to fill days, and more clothes. Plus, the drinking does not begin until après ski. Still, the guys you meet will be total randoms, and they are certain they will never see you again. Just enjoy the skiing and your friends. Enough said.

## Best

### Visit a Friend in Her Hometown

Normal law and order, plus a great opportunity to meet people your friend grew up with... including boys. I might actually sign off on meeting a nice guy that your friend and her family can vouch for, even if he does live somewhere else. As a bonus, her family is around to at least inhibit poor decisions.

# FIRST-DATE NIGHT

### Bad

### Movie

Sitting in a dark room with someone for two hours is not even a date. If he suggests dinner and a movie, just stick to dinner. At least you'll get to know him better that way. Save movie night for once you're a couple.

### Better

### Dinner

This will end up being a great choice *IF* you know he is a good conversationalist, otherwise it can be a long hour or two. Be aware—a Good Guy will always pick up the check. It will just happen, and there will be no question about it. But don't forget to say thank you!

### Best

### Coffee Shop

A perfect place for a first date. You're both clear-headed, you're in a public place and you can either drink lots of coffee (if it's going well) or decide you've had enough (coffee *AND* time with him). Either one can be quite reasonable, depending on how the date's going. This is Dad's Number One choice for a first-date venue.

# EVENTS

## Bad

### Concerts

Going to a concert to meet someone is like going on a date to the movies. Other than a shared interest in the music, there is almost zero chance of learning much more. Also, be careful at all-day music festivals, as drinking, dancing, and not eating all day is a formula for disaster.

## Better

### Football Game

You share an interest, but now you can hear each other (at least most of the time). Just remember, like-mindedness does not always equal Good Man. Beware of overdoing it liquor-wise at the tailgater, though, and keep in mind that that can be a great opportunity to eat something. Last, don't lose your Wingwomen in the crowd.

## Best

### Group Volunteering

There is just no downside to this... and no drinking. Plus, most of the men here get a positive-ledger checkmark for giving of their time for others. Good Guy alert!

# Part VI

# ALWAYS AND NEVER

Wendell Johnson once said *"'Always' and 'Never' are two words you should always remember to never use."* Well, I disagree— here are Dad's absolutes.

# **Always and Never – A Few Absolutes**

Always – Leave your phone's Location Service turned on

Never – Go all the way on a first date

Always – Have a Wingwoman

Never – Accept a ride home with someone when you've been drinking

Always – Keep your wits about you

Never – Let your drink out of your sight

Always – Remember that a Good Man will remain interested tomorrow if you shut him down tonight

Never – Agree to leave the venue with a guy you've just met

Always – Make the time to get a friend home safely

Never – Drink shots

Always – Eat something before you go out

Never – Tell a strange guy where you live

Always – Drink one glass of water between each drink

Never – Drive yourself to any engagement where you might have even *ONE* drink. This ensures you never drive home drunk.

# Part VII

# THE KEY TO ALL GOOD RELATIONSHIPS
## *Love & Happiness*

*"Happiness is having a dream you cannot let go of
and a partner who would never ask you to."*
*– Robert Brault*

*"Let us be grateful to people who make us
happy, they are the charming gardeners
who make our souls blossom."*
*– Marcel Proust*

## Relationships work when your happiness comes before his own... and vice versa. This is the definition of true love.

The reason the words "love" and "happiness" are so often linked is that you can't have one without the other. They should be synonymous and reciprocal, at least in your romantic life. While you might be able to love your best friend or your brother when one of them is doing something that makes you unhappy, you certainly can't say that about your boyfriend or your spouse. It's a different kind of love.

So, let me dispel this notion that love relationships "are a lot of work" (aka "marriage is hard"). This is just an old cliché. If you are in the right relationship, this won't be the case. In fact, all of the happiest couples I know will tell you quite the opposite—their relationship is effortless... marriage is easy.

The key to relationship success lies in each partner's sincerely putting the other's happiness before their own. This leads to a brilliant balance wherein each of you considers the other's feelings before you react to any given circumstance.

For example, if your guy gets invited to play poker on a night that he *knows* he committed to go out with you, the right guy will not even bring up the poker game. Conversely, if he was unaware that you wanted to go out and he checks with you about going to play, your response would naturally be, "Sure, go have fun." This is a bit of an oversimplification, but the idea is that good relationships resolve situations in ways that result in the happiest outcome for both people—not always a perfect outcome, but the best solution all around.

The idea that any good relationship is a lot of work, that you need to be *working* at it, is an idea that was created by marriage counselors to keep their clients in therapy. Good for the counselors. That's how they get paid. Not such a great deal for the couples involved.

If your relationship is "hard" or "work," then you really need to consider the possibility that you are in the wrong relationship. If there is a major imbalance in the give and take, you are not truly prioritizing one another's happiness. You're fighting all the time? Wrong relationship. You constantly need counseling to keep things together? Wrong relationship.

If you're miserable together, go find someone who makes you happy! Life is too short and you owe it to yourself (and each other) to be happy.

## **A little more on the happiness thing...**

You want to find a Good Man who cares deeply about your happiness. I suspect, when you find a guy like this, you will likewise care very deeply about keeping *him* happy. This guy, this "right" guy, will love to see you smile. He will want you to feel good about yourself. His world will revolve around keeping you happy. Not in an insane, obsessive way... but in a wonderful, loving and healthy way.

How will you know? The big things should be obvious, so the place to take note is in the little things. Does he listen to you? Is he interested in what's important to you? Is he patient? Does he hold your hand? Does he do things he knows you enjoy even though he might not like them himself? If so, he's the kind of guy who is demonstrating a capacity to put your happiness before his own.

So here are the traits which will enable him to make, and keep, you happy.

# Part VIII

# WINNERS

## (Characteristics of a Good Man)

## You Can Find Good Men Anywhere

I am sure one of the reasons you're reading this book is to have me tell you where and how to find a Good Man. I wish I could tell you, but the reality is that you can find good men anywhere. The surprising part is probably that the "usual" good places you hear about are really no guarantee at all. Church? No. In my experience being church-going or religious has very little to do with the most important factors in being a Good Man. Business school? Not necessarily. There are plenty of successful and well-educated Losers out there. While shopping at Target? Hey, maybe so.

Finding a Good Man has everything to do with what he's like on the inside. Not what he does. Not where he works. Not where he hangs out. Does he need to have a job? Absolutely... or at least be looking for one. Does he need a moral compass? Of course. But what I want you to recognize is that a nice-looking pedigree or affiliation with a certain organization should not automatically make you think he's a decent guy.

Good men can come from anywhere and from any background. The proper credentials for being a Good Man cross all socioeconomic boundaries. What I hope to lay out in this next section of the book is a list of indicators for a sincere, trustworthy, and worthwhile guy and how to spot them.

Good men *are* out there. You just have to be patient and observant. Much as with spotting a Loser, when you know the traits of a champion, he will become increasingly apparent to you. A Good Man will keep you happy for the rest of your life. Isn't that worth working for?

---

## *SOMETHING ELSE...*

A Good Man makes *YOU* a stronger, better person!

---

# # 1

## LOYALTY AND TRUST

*"Achievement of your happiness is the
only moral purpose of your life...
since it is the proof and the result of your
loyalty to the achievement of your values."
– Ayn Rand*

*"To be trusted is a greater compliment
than being loved."
– George MacDonald*

These two ideals (along with Discipline and Self-control, covered in the next chapter) comprise the core essentials of a good man. His ability to be loyal and true is what you are pinning your future hopes on. Without loyalty and trust, there is no foundation on which to build a real relationship. I am taking it for granted that you can be loyal and true—now you need to find the same capacities in your guy. Every guy I've ever known would tell you he's loyal and trustworthy. But how do you know that it's true?

In this area, actions will always speak louder than words. Look first to his friends and family. How does he demonstrate these characteristics in his interactions with, and his discussions about, those he already should hold dear? Does he stand by them through thick and thin? Does he take the time to be there for them, even if it involves some sacrifice? A Good Man will drop everything to be there for his friends and family. The right guy will not badmouth those he loves.

How does he react when he sees disloyalty in others? It should be intolerable to him. How does he judge others who have betrayed his trust? Harshly. It is all about standards, and his must be *demonstrably* high. It is not enough to talk a big game in this department, you must see that he walks the walk.

### A couple more positive indicators in this department:

- Does he follow through when he has given his word?
- Is he known for "doing business with a handshake"?
- Does he have a reputation for honesty and integrity at work? Among his peers?

- Does he surround himself with people who have proven to be trustworthy?
- What do his friends say about him?
- Do any of his past relationships indicate difficult but consistent decisions around violation of his trust?

## A Quick Bit about Men Being Selfish

If you didn't know it already, men are unbelievably selfish creatures. Left to our own devices, we would do nothing but what we want, when we want all the time. We *LOVE* our hobbies. We *LOVE* our games. We *LOVE* our free time. We *LOVE* our routines. That is why we are such creatures of habit. We fall in love with what we like, and we never grow tired of indulging in those things.

As difficult as it is for you girls to hear, women are just a small part of a man's selfish world. We enjoy having sex with you because it's pleasurable... and we're selfish. This element works out great for us. More difficult is remaining engaged in the other aspects of the relationship, especially those parts which are not particularly interesting to men. Like shopping. Or cleaning house. Or listening to your friends' problems.

In the early stages of a new relationship with any man, you will be the focus of his attention because he is interested in you. *YOU* are in his self-interest at that moment, so it should not be at all surprising that any new guy can focus on you. This is easy for all men. We are masters of the early stages of a relationship because we *WANT* something from you. Once we've caught you, we will tend to fall back to the parts of the relationship we want. Again, that's the easy part. The question is, can he keep from sliding back too far into selfish behavior over time as the new-car smell wears off your relationship?

# # 2

# DISCIPLINE AND SELF-CONTROL

*"In reading the lives of great men, I found
that the first victory they won
was over themselves... self-discipline
with all of them came first."
– Harry S. Truman*

*"Happiness is dependent on self-discipline.
We are the biggest obstacles to our own happiness."
– Dennis Prager*

Along with loyalty and trust, discipline and self-control are the other two must-have traits in a Good Man. Because men are selfish, it takes discipline to avoid reverting to our pre-relationship ways. There will be a tendency, over time, for us to return to our "true selves." In other words, if we never did the dishes in our single lives but were very helpful with the dishes in order to impress you, the girl we want to score with, it is quite likely you'll find us no longer being helpful with the dishes once we're in a relationship.

You want a man who will generally do the right thing even if that is not the easy thing... especially if you know he is sacrificing something he'd much rather be doing. Does he do what's right *ESPECIALLY* when that is not what's easy?

A disciplined man should be able to set his mind to anything reasonable and see it through to the end. Challenge him to a contest of will and see how he does. Discipline is what will keep him focused on the right priorities for you and your future together. Discipline is what will keep him fit. Discipline is what will keep him getting up early and looking for work when he's out of a job. Discipline is what will get him the promotion that will increase your standard of living. Discipline is what will allow him to save money even though it would be much more fun to spend it on one of his favorite things, such as tickets to a game with his buddies.

You want to see some discipline in all aspects of his life. Not to the point where he becomes a dull boy, but definitely the willpower to get things done when it matters. Doing what's right versus what's easy should be a given with your man. If something is important, there won't be any corner-cutting. He will do it right.

Hand-in-hand with discipline comes self-control. They are related but different. Self-control helps men control impulsiveness—and impulsive guys often make mistakes. Now, a little impulsiveness is fine... and sometimes great fun. But it's the loss of self-control that leads to *BIG* impulsive mistakes. That's what you have to watch out for. Does he go a bit overboard when he's holiday shopping? OK. Does he buy a big-screen TV you can't afford when you're already struggling to make rent? Problem!

A great indicator of self-control is the ability to delay gratification. Can your man wait? This is not about the little things, like can he keep from snitching a cookie, but more significant demonstrations of being able to wait—like can he wait for sex if it is important to you. And can he wait patiently, or is he a jerk about it?

Loss of self-control can also lead to many other problems: gambling, drinking, abuse, credit card debt… cheating. See if your man can walk away from situations when they are becoming difficult. Can he stop drinking when he needs to? Can he get up from the blackjack table when he has lost what he could afford to lose? If he can, then he's the kind of guy who can also walk away from other temptations, and that is what you want to see in your guy.

---

## A Good Man Would Ace the Marshmallow Test

In the late '60s, Stanford Professor Walter Mischel ran an experiment in delayed gratification known as the Marshmallow Test. Basically these studies offered young children the opportunity to have a single marshmallow right away or wait a short time (roughly 15 minutes) and receive *TWO* marshmallows. Not surprisingly the experiment revealed that those who could wait for the extra reward went on to have better life outcomes, including test scores, educational achievements and lower body mass indexes.

A Good Man should be able to pass the Marshmallow Test easily if *YOU* are the reward at the end of the wait!

# # 3

# COACHABLE

*"How can you improve if you're never wrong?"*
*– Pat Summitt*

A related trait that warrants its own heading is Coachability. An ideal guy has enough ego that he likes to win, but not so much that he can't see the need to up his game. This self-reflection on performance and recognition of room to improve is pretty rare in the male gender. Any man who has it is going to be more adaptable and responsive. He is also very likely already a winner in whatever he undertakes.

Of course, being Coachable also requires a modicum of discipline, hence the note here. I don't want this trait to, in any way, make you think men are readily *CHANGEABLE*... this is not the case. Coachable means being able to redirect and focus strengths. Coachable guys like to win. Winning your heart means making you happy. Making you happy is what it's all about.

A great indicator of Coachability that every woman will smile about? Can he ask for directions? Boom! Coachable!

# # 4

## THOUGHTFUL *vs.* SENSITIVE

*"It makes me want to be more thoughtful.
I have to try to treat people right the
first time around". – Penn Jillette*

Despite what you'll read in women's magazines and hear on the wish lists of many girls, men are not built to be sensitive. We are just not wired that way. Sensitive is defined (by Google) as "having or displaying a quick and delicate appreciation of others' feelings." I think women often pick up on unspoken cues from others better than men do, and they expect men to have a similar, almost ESP-like ability to know when something is up. This is not men at all.

Have you ever been around a couple when the man finds out his mate has been mad at him for a while and he has no idea? Women think that guy is an idiot. How could he *NOT* have known?! Well, did she tell him? I mean actually speak up and say it, outloud, to his face? Probably not. He is likely being sincere. When these types of things happen, we men usually have no clue. You have to tell us, or we will just keep rolling... oblivious. Don't expect your man to pick up on the unspoken. That would be sensitive... and we aren't.

What you *CAN* reasonably expect of a good man is to be thoughtful... and when I say "thoughtful," I mean when you make him *AWARE* of something, he should react in a meaningful way. Let's circle back with the comparison here and use a real-life situation.

Let's say you are having a terrible week at work and your body language is screaming this to the world. Your guy might not do anything. He might not even notice. Insensitive? Yes, but not unexpected. However, if you tell him, "I am having the shittiest week of my life," and your guy doesn't bring you flowers...or make dinner...or draw you a bubble bath, then he's not *THOUGHTFUL*. He is now aware you are struggling and he has failed to react. This is bad. Not thoughtful means not making your happiness a priority—and this means he's not a keeper.

A good man can and should be expected to be thoughtful... maybe not perfectly, but at least most of the time.

# # 5

## HE CAN APOLOGIZE AND
## OWN HIS MISTAKES

*"More people should apologize,
and more people should
accept apologies when sincerely made."*
*– Greg LeMond*

This one is self-explanatory. A good man knows when he was wrong and will act accordingly. Don't force him to apologize—he should get there on his own. A simple and heartfelt "I'm sorry" might be one of the best indicators that you've found a keeper.

If and when this happens, forgive him... and mean it!

If you've never seen the movie *Jerry Maguire*, you should watch it and check out the apology he drops at the end... followed by his wife's amazing response. Good stuff.

You should be able to spot this trait pretty easily. Men who don't blame others for their shortcomings and have a buck-stops-here mentality are good bets to be able to ask for forgiveness, too. Just *NEVER* accept an apology on a Dealbreaker (remember that list?) and make sure he doesn't prove to be Always Sorry, Never Learn Guy.

# # 6

# DOES HE KNOW WHAT MATTERS TO YOU?

*"I have learned that only two things are
necessary to keep one's wife happy.
First, let her think she's having her own
way. And second, let her have it."*
*– Lyndon B. Johnson*

The right kind of man will shape his behavior to demonstrate he understands what is important to you. If you value tidiness, he should make an effort to be more tidy. If you love the theater, he will go with you. He doesn't have to be a genius, but should clearly show an aptitude for knowing when and when not to bring up wanting to go out on his own (for that poker game or whatever).

This is a significant qualifier—ask *vs.* tell. Regardless of the stage of your relationship, he should be tactful enough to phrase his plans in the form of a question. It will indicate that he knows your first preference is that he spends time with you. Everything else is time away. All smart men know that women keep a secret ledger of time spent off doing guy stuff. Asking is just the indicator he knows you're letting him go. So, set some reasonable parameters and let him go play with his buddies.

The very smart guy will also know when he has asked to go out too often. He won't even push that far... at least not after the first couple of times. This goes back to being Coachable.

# # 7

## GUYS WHO'VE BEEN CHEATED ON

*"The emotion that can break your heart is
sometimes the very one that heals it."
– Nicholas Sparks*

You do not want to be the immediate rebound date
for this guy. However, after some time has gone by to
heal wounds, the guy who has been cheated on can
actually be a pretty nice catch. The Good Man who
has had his heart broken can become even more loyal,
thoughtful and detail-oriented. Good Men usually
don't get cheated on, but it does happen. And then all
their good habits really end up reinforcing themselves
after they recover.

Another good indicator that he's the Good type is
how he looks at his ex-wife or girlfriend. Good Men
value and expect loyalty in return, so being cheated
on should make their ex damaged goods forever. It's
not that they might not miss their ex—that might be
normal for a short time. It is that, in their hearts, they
know they would never take her back. Betrayal is a
Dealbreaker for them, too.

# # 8

## GUYS WHO HAVE SISTERS

*"One thing that has helped me to
become patient and cool
is that I grew up with sisters." – William Kamkwamba*

*"I saw how my sister got treated by
boyfriends. I read this thing that said
in a relationship with a woman, imagine
how you would feel if you were
her father. That's been my approach, for
the most part." – Orlando Bloom*

This might be one of the greatest indicators of all time. Men who grew up with sisters have, generally, picked up good habits and have almost certainly witnessed the fallout of their siblings' relationships that have gone bad. These guys tend to be more aware of how to treat women properly and respectfully. So, the more sisters, the better—especially older sisters.

This, of course, assumes your guy is close with his sisters. The more distant, the less positive the correlation is likely to be. The added bonus of a tight-knit family with one or more sisters is that his behavior will almost certainly be monitored—and commented on—by his female siblings. This is very much to your benefit.

You can also glean some insights by cozying up to your man's sisters. They will almost always give you the dirt on his past relationships and expound on any shortcomings their brother might have. Ask good questions... and react accordingly. A sister's perspective will almost certainly be biased, but the circumstances of his past situations should be indicative of future performance.

The bottom line is... moms may let their boys get away with bad behavior. Past girl friends, too. Sisters? No way!

# # 9

## OTHER FAMILY

*"A child who is allowed to be
disrespectful to his parents
will not have true respect for anyone." – Billy Graham*

*"For a man, there's a big responsibility
that comes with having a boy
because men are made by their fathers." – Rafe Spall*

If your guy treats his mom well, that's a great sign. For one, it means he was raised to have an appropriate respect and appreciation for her—and, most likely, for all women. Core principles and values are always grounded in upbringing, so you should be eager to meet his family as soon as you know you like him.

Good Man behavior and a healthy attitude toward women are often learned from the father, though. If your guy's mother is still married, watch how his father treats his mother. Good dad does not always equal good son, but it is a pretty solid bet.

Conversely, any hatred toward mom or dad needs to be checked out pretty quickly. This should be a red flag until you can substantiate the reason for it.

# # 10

## HOW HE TREATS OTHERS

*"Treat others as you want to be
treated." – The Golden Rule*

*"Never lose sight of the fact that the most
important yardstick of your success
will be how you treat other people—your
family, friends, and co-workers,
and even strangers you meet along
the way." – Barbara Bush*

There is also lots of stuff to glean about your man's character from his interaction with those outside his family: friends, co-workers, and especially those who serve him.

Friends can be placed in a tier just below sisters in terms of strategy and information. Friends are least likely to spill the dirt, but also very likely to expound on his best traits. The more friends who recognize the same, positive characteristics, the more those ring true. You can also pick up on habits which you may or may not be able to live with long-term. Friends will know if he's punctual, reliable, thrifty, etc.

Co-workers are valuable for assessing his work ethic and reliability, but even more revealing is how he treats this group of people who are not friends, but acquaintances. Everyone has co-workers they like and others they dislike. How does he handle those he dislikes? Can he still get work done? Can he persevere? Work is not always fun, and how he handles work, especially with those who are not fun can speak volumes as to how he will handle "un-fun" situations with you moving forward.

Finally, there are the people throughout his day who provide services. How does he treat the woman at the coffee counter? The guy who sells him tires? I believe the best indicator of a person's true character comes in how they treat those who serve them. You want a guy who is appreciative, engaged, and demonstrates his appreciation. This is especially important in assessing a boyfriend who grew up in a life of privilege. Any man who treats service people like servants is not worth two cents. Any person who treats service personnel like inferiors should be dumped immediately.

In marriage, you are vowing to serve one another for the rest of your days. Make sure that it will be *SERVING*, not his treating you like a servant. You do not want to be treated like a servant by anybody, but especially not by the man you love.

# # 11

## VOLUNTEERISM AND HELPING
## THOSE IN NEED

*"It is more blessed to give than to receive." – Jesus*

*"I think a gentleman is someone who holds the comfort
of other people above [his] own." —Anna Kendrick*

Here is another chapter which is pretty much self-
explanatory. Those who give of themselves, especially
to complete strangers, always give even more to those
they know... and more still to those they love. Giving
your time in the service of others is selfless—exactly
what you're looking for. You want a guy with a big heart.

Even better, see if he shows up *particularly* when he
doesn't want to. He will not let others down even when
he really would like to. A commitment is a commitment
and, if he treats it that way, he has real integrity.

# # 12

## MODESTY

*"He who speaks without modesty will find
it difficult to make his words good."
– Confucius*

Not to be confused with lacking in confidence, showing Modesty is a good indicator your man is comfortable with who he is. It also keeps him out of several of the Loser categories. As you build your lives together, you want to build it with a guy who recognizes it's not all about him... that you are doing it together. A Modest man will express his appreciation for those who are helping them do the lifting, not draw attention to his own strength.

Look for an athlete who credits his teammates or coach, a leader who salutes his team, a student who cites his teachers. Of course, if you meet a devout man, he might also deflect praise to the Lord.

# # 13

## SENSE OF HUMOR

*"A sense of humor is needed armor. Joy
in one's heart and some laughter
on one's lips is a sign that the person down
deep has a pretty good grasp of life."*
*– Hugh Sidey*

As a man who likes to laugh myself, it will not surprise you to see Humor on my Good Guy qualifiers. Most lists I see of qualities women desire in their mates includes this trait at or near the top. With good reason. If you want to be happy, find a happy man... and I don't know any happy men who do not have a sense of humor. I really believe this is one of the best indicators you could ask for, especially if he also throws in the occasional self-deprecating jab. He should laugh easily, even at himself.

It goes without saying he can't just be funny and never take anything seriously, but that should be a very easy distinction to make.

As an added bonus, humor has a positive effect on women's health because it helps de-escalate conflict, according to Regina Boyle Wheeler of Everyday Health.com.

# # 14

## CHIVALRY

*"[My mom] taught me how to appreciate and*
*respect women. She taught me chivalry*
*and how to love a woman and respect*
*[her] feelings and emotions."*
*– Shemar Moore*

---

### Dad's Note about Chivalry

*In this day and age of gender equality, these*
*"old-fashioned" gestures of deference*
*have fallen away as men's fear of appearing*
*sexist overcomes the desire to be polite.*

---

Chivalry is a Good Man trait that's actually easy to spot. It's the guy who opens the door and allows you to go in first, the guy who makes sure you're seated first, the one who helps you on with your coat—and a million other little things that signal good manners and an awareness of others. He's the polar opposite of the tedious "me-first" dude who's just positive he's the center of the universe.

Guys who have a sense of chivalry are often Good Men for two reasons. First, they learned chivalrous behavior somewhere, which is a great indicator they were raised with a positive role model, probably their dad. Secondly, it means they know how to treat a woman. While some might deem this old-fashioned, I am telling you it is a trait that will always make you, as a woman, feel special. A few years ago, I saw the then-boyfriend of a cousin out shoveling her sidewalks after a snow. I commented to my girls, "That's a Good Man there, out shoveling Brooke's walk early in the freezing cold." He was. They're now happily married.

Actually, when you get right down to it, chivalry really is nothing more than good manners. Why would you want to put up with someone who has a deficit in this department? Incidentally, if you think he overdoes things a bit in the chivalry department, simply request that he take it down a notch... then you'll know if he's Coachable, as well!

---

### Examples of Chivalrous Behavior

Holding the door for you (and others)
Walking you to the door after a date
Offering his coat when you are cold
Letting you order first (your server
SHOULD have this nailed also)
Helping you on and off with your jacket
Speaking strongly if you are disrespected
Waiting for you to begin eating

Offering his seat to a woman on
a crowded bus or train
Helping carry things when your hands are full
Waiting for you to be seated
Offering to escort you safely after dark

---

# # 15

## DESIRE TO MAKE IT RIGHT

A Good Man is going to want to fix things when he knows something is not right. This is not "fix things" as in repair broken stuff around the apartment, this is fix things as in set things right in your relationship. If he asks you what's wrong, that is a very good sign. Do him a favor at this point—tell him what's bugging you. There is nothing more frustrating to a Good Man than to realize you're mad, ask what's the matter, and then have you reply, "Nothing."

# # 16

## THE LITTLE THINGS

This brings me to a good indicator of a Good Man and a brilliant indicator of a shrewd man—the unexpected flowers... or latte... or dessert. If a guy brings you flowers or some other little something, for no reason other than he was "thinking of you," it means you've found a guy who actually managed to step out of his selfish time and think about your happiness. He probably wasn't thinking of you in the daydream sense. He was thinking about your reaction when he sees you later. That's why he got the flowers, he knew they would make you happy!

# # 17

## "REVEALS" VIA EX-GIRLFRIENDS

First of all, he better not have a whole bunch of them, exes. This is a Good Man we're talking about, so it should be a cautionary note to you if he's broken lots of hearts or been dumped a bunch of times. It's hard to quantify how many is too many, so just let your intuition guide you.

Pay close attention to how your guy speaks about his past relationships. There are many things you can glean from his reflections. Is he angry? Resentful? Introspective? Remember that, like it or not, he was in a relationship with this woman prior to you. Does he say she was crazy? Are his comments cruel or mean? Even if she broke his heart, how does his tone reflect on him? He cared about her at some point. Does he acknowledge that?

Better yet, can he also be insightful about his own contribution to the demise of the relationship. He doesn't have to own the breakup, but they are almost always two-way streets. If and how he recalls things to you can tell you a lot about his character and give you helpful glimpses into both the Good and Loser elements of his personality.

## *Dad Would Rather...*

You Marry a Kind Guy
than
A Smart Guy

# # 18

## HE'S ALREADY A PROVEN FRIEND

*"Girls, I'm going to let you in on a little secret
you haven't been letting yourself believe:
9 out of 10 guys only become your best friend
so that they can date you." – Jon Negroni*

Last but not least, do not discount the guy who is already your friend. Just as you grow to like someone, it is also very possible to grow more attracted to someone. My first serious relationship developed in exactly this way. We hung around together in the same extended group. Over time, we came to know and respect each other's upbringings and values. We started hanging out, just the two of us. And over time, we came around to being attracted and romantically involved. Our friends didn't even know, and it was actually kind of fun keeping it secret for a while.

Anyway, the point is, sometimes the Good Man is right there in front of you, and maybe you just need to look at him with fresh eyes. And the bonus is—if there ends up being a spark, at least you can roll forward knowing he's not a Loser.

# Part IX

# 12 Things
# FOR KEEPING A GOOD
# MAN HAPPY

I am always amazed when women can't
understand the following key basics about
men. Knowing and understanding these things
will help you keep your Good Man happy
and make you look like the coolest girl ever.

### Thing 1
**Put His Happiness before Your Own**

Always open yourself up to this gradually (since you need to establish he's a Good Man), but this is the Golden Rule of keeping both of you happy. This was covered earlier, but I mention it again here because it should always be Numero Uno with both of you. Also, keep in mind, his happiness will occasionally involve doing things without you... and *THAT'S OK!* Tell him it's OK. And mean it!

### Thing 2
**Men Enjoy Having Sex**

While this is qualified in the Conventional Wisdom section "Men Have Needs," we are going on the assumption that you've established he's a Good Man. Being into him, and especially being into having sex with him, is really important. The physical connection for men is at least as significant as the emotional one. Don't let other things get in the way of being together. It's hugely important.

### Thing 3
**Initiate Intimacy and Fun**

Piggybacking on the previous chapter, guys are usually charged with initiating everything, be it contact, sex, whatever. Make it easier. As covered earlier in the book, we are not mind readers. Let us know when you're ready to make out, have fun. Your guy will appreciate it and love you for it.

Better yet, buy some lingerie. Surprise him when you wear it. Sometimes women equate lingerie with trashy men's magazines. "That's slutty." And they are half-right. Do you know why models in men's magazines wear lingerie? Because men like it! If you're comfortable wearing it, then *DO IT!* We're visual creatures and lingerie is a great picture frame. Think of it as gift-wrapping!

## Thing 4
### "Soul Mate" and "Best Friend" Silliness

These are awful concepts that some overzealous women came up with. It's girl-talk. It's not reality. Your man wants you to be his woman. His girlfriend. His wife. You are not his "soul mate." This is sappy Hallmark-card lingo based on an idea that's even more absurd— you are the only woman out of literally billions who is a match for him. As if! Making him call you his soul mate is dumb... and makes you seem like you need reassurance.

A Good Man could have ended up in any number of great circumstances with someone else just like you. Take comfort in knowing it's you, and be glad it's you.. but it's unseemly and insipid to try to make him feel like it could *only* have been you.

Very similar is making your man feel like you need to be his "best friend." Let's acknowledge (or hope) that he has at least one male relationship that he's developed over his entire lifetime that's achieved "best friend" status before you came along. You should embrace that friend. You should encourage that friendship. It is important to your man. That guy is his best friend—you are *NOT* his best friend. You are *MORE* than that and always will be. You are the woman he loves. Be content with that and let him have a real best friend, too.

If your boyfriend or husband reads this and still insists that you are truly his best friend, then one of two things is true: 1) he is a Loser who was unable to build even one meaningful male relationship in his life, or 2) you drove away his social connections outside your relationship and you need to *IMMEDIATELY* encourage him to get out and reconnect. If it has become all about you, you have already severely violated Thing #1 above!

As an added bonus, you want him to have a best friend so you can *MEET* the guy and further establish your Good Man's credentials. Another bonus: his best friend might also prove to be a great find for your single friends—who knows?!

### Thing 5
### All Men Notice Other Women

He's a Good Man. Let him look. He's not going anywhere and you do not need to be jealous or act offended. Women who begrudge their men a peek at a good-looking woman (or the *Sports Illustrated* swimsuit issue, for instance) just make themselves look petty. Believe me, when guys get together and talk about wives and girlfriends, we all know who's gotten himself stuck with one of these types. Don't be her.

### Thing 6
### Avoid the No-win Questions

Please don't ask us questions like, "Does this dress look OK?" Our answer will always be yes. Regardless. The same goes for something like, "Do you think she's pretty?" Our answer will always be "no" or "not as pretty as you." When your follow-up to our reply is "Are you sure?", you have put us in an impossible spot. Stop it.

### Thing 7
### Just Answer Our Questions, Already!

Now when we ask questions, just tell us straight up. If your man asks what you feel like for dinner, don't say, "Whatever you feel like" or "Anything's fine." Nine times out of ten it's not and you know it. More importantly, *WE* know it. That's why we asked *YOU*. Please don't make us go through the process of naming restaurants and cuisines until you stop making the that's-not-it face. This applies to all of these types of queries about movies, food, etc. If we're asking you, we really don't care what we end up doing, just as long as the decision gets made...*now*.

## Thing 8
### Men Are Like Little Kids

This rule means to keep three things in mind:

1. Be patient, especially if we're acting immature.
2. Reward us when we demonstrate good behavior.
3. Sometimes suggest a playdate with a friend without being asked.

## Thing 9
### Even Good Men Are Selfish

We're men, too, after all. Respect our routines, as they are important to us. And allow room for at least one reasonable hobby that doesn't involve you. We love you but do not want to be with you 24-7.

And here's another thing—learn to pick your fights. Not everything, every little difference of opinion, is worth arguing about. If something's really, really important to you, then take a stand. If not, then let it go. You'll both be much happier.

## Thing 10
### Even the Best Men Behave Poorly Occasionally

If it is habitual, then your man is a Loser. But even the best of men have occasional lapses. As long as it is not a Dealbreaking transgression (cheating, abuse, violation of trust), try to forgive him his slip-up as quickly and benevolently as possible. He will be greatly relieved and love you all the more for it.


### **Thing 11**
### **Sometimes You Are Out of Sight and Out of Mind**

When he's off having fun (ideally on a junket you supported), remember that he will not be thinking of you... and that's because he's a man. It's OK. He still loves you. He might have so much fun he even forgets to call. *IT'S OK!*

In the meantime, you can use your free time to enjoy yourself. Visit with girlfriends or just stay in and paint your toenails—whatever makes you happy—things that you never have time for when he's around. Then it becomes a win-win for both of you. All good!


### **Thing 12**
### **Be Appreciative**

Let him know you appreciate his effort, especially if he's being thoughtful. Maybe even more significant, thank him when he tries but fails in his attempts to fix things. When the intention is good, this will reinforce the thought, versus the outcome.

Being appreciative also helps him remember how great *YOU* are and makes him more expressive of his thanks for all you do. Mutual happiness—name of the game!

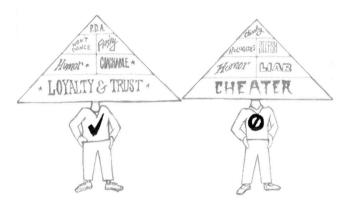

# Part X

# AN IMPORTANT ANALOGY:
## The Man-Trait Pyramid

# **Men Are Like the Food Pyramid**

Men, like our fine governmental nutritional guidelines, are not composed of just one complete type of guy. Each guy you meet will have a combination of the characteristics outlined in this book. The key for you is to figure out what comprises the bulk of your man's character. What lies at the base of his pyramid? Any guy who has a quality foundation is going to probably be worth getting to know better. Conversely, any guy with a Loser foundation is going to be trouble, despite a smattering of good stuff up where the pyramid gets skinny.

It is critical to discern character accurately, as many Losers can show signs of potential... and even have some very endearing traits. But you have to remain strong. A flawed base is never going to hold up over time.

Of course, any man's pyramid which has even the smallest element of The Cheater, is flawed in full, even if every single other good element is present. One bit of The Cheater turns the whole thing to sand. Ditto for The Abuser. Or any of the Dealbreakers.

Just remember to be a little bit open-minded on the stuff that's not on the Dealbreaker list. Even most Good Guys, no different from women, are unlikely to be perfect. Odds are pretty good that your eventual Mr. Right is actually going to have one or two things that are not on your ideal-man list. If he makes you happy, though, they will be easy to overlook.

# CONCLUSION

## So Now You Know

*"If you haven't found it yet, keep looking. Don't settle. As with all matters of the heart, you'll know when you find it. And, like any great relationship, it just gets better and better as the years roll on." – Steve Jobs*

So now you know just about all the secrets this dad knows about his fellow man. I know that I am going to take a good deal of grief for giving up the dirt on my brethren, but if it leads to you finding a Good Man of your own, I will gladly suffer the consequences. In closing, I want to qualify everything I have written here with the following:

- With each new relationship remain optimistic. You never know when a really Good Man might cross your path. Just be careful and aware of the percentages. You ladies are too hopeful. You tend to return from every first date thinking, "He could be the one." Single women really need to approach every new man with a healthy dose of realism. Odds are very good he is *NOT* the one. So, try to temper your enthusiasm until he proves otherwise.

- When I say "most men are losers," I'm obviously referring to the majority, and this correlates with a point along the age scale. In high school, all guys are pretty much available, so the field is wide open. By age 40, however, there are simply far fewer unattached men—especially Good Men because they have already taken themselves out of the dating pool. Of course, men re-circulate due to various life changes, but the pool of Good Men has definitely narrowed.

- This creates a gender advantage for men, but certainly not an impossible one to surmount. I know many happy couples who met in their 40s... and even later. The main thing is to be wide awake and open to possibilities so you can recognize your Good Man when he turns up.

- A Good Man will prove to be just that over time. Make him prove he is the exception. That is what he will be doing for the rest of your life!

- If you suspect a guy is a Loser, then *HE IS!* Be decisive and dump him.

- Men are crafty. If a guy you're dating ever reads this, don't be surprised if he adapts to better sell himself. Never underestimate men. We're simple... but not stupid.

- Be happy! Men love happy women.

- There is a good one out there waiting to meet you—so always be open and ready.

- Remember, men are like the food pyramid—as long as you have a good base, you can get away with some stuff that's a little bad for you at the top.

- If you like a guy, make *SURE* he knows. It should be subtle, but it should be clear. If you are certain he knows and he still doesn't do anything, then he is not interested in you. End of story.

- Never, *EVER* feel the need to settle.

So, go out there tomorrow with your eyes wide open. Be yourself, be open, and be fun. Just be careful, for your sake... and your dad's.

# A Personal Note: How Did I Get Here?

## *(A Little Background on Dad)*

Having read this dissertation on the Loserdom of Man, I am sure you have asked yourself more than a couple of times, "Has he always been on his high horse, or is he a reformed Loser speaking from experience?" The truth is my perspective comes from a little bit of both.

I was raised in a yes-ma'am/no-ma'am household by awesome parents who remain married to this day. They were great role models for a loving and happy relationship, and my dad taught me from childhood that you treat women well. I got to witness lots of alcoholism—and its consequences, though. It was on my dad's side of the family, a genetic predisposition that was transferred wholly to my generation, too.

I had a very close relationship with my older sister, who was an invaluable mentor. Like many young women, she fell in and out of love many times growing up, and I was there to observe all the consequences. She would share her thoughts on relationships and dating, and I was a very coachable kid, so I listened to her and tried to incorporate her lessons into my dating game plan.

I was a Play the Field Guy in high school, always being pretty up front about not wanting a serious relationship. I was completely spoiled with opportunity, as there were lots of pretty and fun girls to go out with, and I tried to date all of them. While I was a bit of a gadabout, I wasn't a complete scoundrel, and my mother's voice in the back of my head kept my virginity intact through graduation.

College was a bit of a shock to my system. After dating anyone and everyone in my high school, freshman year at Stanford proved to be a dating wasteland. I spent most of my time drinking beer at parties and marveling at the handful of cute girls being preyed upon by the upperclassmen. I was so outraged at some of the rough treatment visited upon my female dorm mates that I actually had a couple of fistfights with the Losers who abused them.

Sophomore year I fell in love for the first time. I was so darn thankful to have landed a cute and all-around awesome girlfriend that I found myself, for the first time, working to keep someone other than Mark Berzins happy. I effectively applied many lessons learned by this point in my life—loyalty, trust, thoughtfulness— with great results. The few ripples in our relationship were also entirely my fault... and basically always drinking-related.

We stayed together after graduation even though we worked in different cities. At some point along the way, we mutually agreed that it would be smart and healthy to meet other people in order to validate our decision that we were the right match. The qualifier was that if either of us might discover a new relationship we wanted to pursue romantically, we would tell the other. I thought this was a very grown-up combination of belief in myself and trust in her. I was confident—turns out overconfident—in my value to her as a Good Man.

I found out, months later, that she was seeing someone else. I had to drag it out of her. I was utterly devastated, especially because I knew *MY* values—trust, loyalty— would never allow me to forgive her. We never spoke again. While it did not excuse her unforgivable betrayal (Dealbreaker), some part of me knew that the chink in my armor must have been my bad habits, especially the drinking.

But like a complete Loser, I didn't reign in my partying ways. In fact, I cranked things up a notch. I also decided to become a man-whore. In the target-rich environment of Manhattan Beach, I rolled through women like a man on a mission. I hung out with Men Drinking in Groups, and we all behaved badly. I didn't find anyone remotely interesting but, then again, who would have wanted to capture the attention of a guy acting like such a jerk.

Eventually, I came back to Denver to visit friends and was introduced to my future wife by my best friend and his fiancé. She was her sister, and they were certain we would hit it off. We went on a double date and they were right—I was completely smitten.

The coachable me knew that I needed to be better this time around. I had lost out on my first love, so I needed to bring more self-control to my bad habits. I gave up chewing tobacco (I know—yuck) and reigned in my drinking, pretty much overnight. I committed to her early, so she knew I was all-in.

It worked. 23 years later, I am happier than ever. I know my wife is, too. It has shocked me how effortless our relationship has been. You can thank her for all the Keep a Good Man Happy tips. I still battle my Selfish Guy moments every day.

We moved back to Denver and started Little Pub Company in 1994. I worked behind the bar for the next six years and came to witness countless Loser moments from men. Similarly, I must have listened to a thousand stories from young female employees and customers about men behaving badly. Through counseling them, I came to recognize the prevalence of Losers in the dating pool, which led to raising my girls with those lessons in mind... which then led to this book.

# Acknowledgements

I couldn't have gotten this thing done without the help and encouragement of so many people.

Other than my wife and daughters, I have to thank Rachel Greenwald for steering me in the right direction so this idea could become a reality.

Secondly, a big thank-you to my focus group: Jordan, Madeleine, Amelia, Adelita, Kate, Ursula, Brittany, Meghan, Trish, Susie, Christine, Carolyn, Terry, Hanne, and Kelly.

Finally, to my editor, Nancy Hutchins and my illustrator, Marc Huebert, my gratitude for helping me through the finishing touches.

CPSIA information can be obtained at www.ICGtesting.com
Printed in the USA
LVOW10s0249300615

444382LV00001B/8/P